ROAD TO NAKA-IMA

ROAD TO NAKA-IMA

A Man's Journey to a New Civilization

Stuart A. Bernstein

cassiquiare press

Cover design and illustration
by Eric Auer, Aspen, Colorado

Acknowledgments

This book would not have been possible without my parents, my brother, and everyone who followed. What perfection our lives embrace. Thank you one and all.

It was my life partner, Mary, however, who saw the way for the individual stories to coalesce. She provided the envelope for the writing. She polished it, made sense out of chaos, and disposed of what was too self-absorbed. She provided the vital balance, the yin to embrace and soften my yang.

Mary's assessment of my work was always appropriate, occasionally painful, and ultimately liberating for me. She welcomed the most minor of revisions as a practice in impeccability.

Her support for me and for this book has been unconditional. Truly, I am blessed to be with her. And we have only begun.

Contents

Part One

Introduction

Once upon a time, I contemplated writing a novel. It would be a gripping fantasy-adventure taking place in some tumultuous present-future. I imagined two men and their families thrown into an epic journey, the outcome upon which the very future of humankind would pivot.

The men, one an Arab, the other a Jew, would meet as classmates at a unique school of healing. They would share an intense and competitive love-hate relationship.

One day, years after each had practiced their extraordinary form of healing and brought it to mastery, they would be called out on a mission of universal consequence. It would be a rite of passage for the men, their wives, and their children, with severe repercussions for all if they failed. At every turn, metaphysical lessons revealing universal laws would arise, mostly transmitted by unearthly enlightened ones. And, oh . . . the bad guys would of course be terrible in a larger-than-life way.

Woven into the story would be factual information, mythology, and ancient prophecies about the time we are entering. I would include numerological revelations recently extracted from the Bible: By taking every fifth, seventh, or fiftieth letter from the Old Testament, ancient prophecies about events in the course of our civilization have been revealed, including accurate name, place, and date predictions from the entire course of this epoch. I would bring in prophecies based upon the ancient Shinto and Mayan calendars, which I'm told predict the end of this civilization at the very same moment less than twenty years from now.

The families would run dangerous rivers, climb mountains, ski across forbidding terrain, and face death at every turn. The closer they came to their objective, the meaner and more formidable their enemies would become.

Somewhere, probably in Utah, the ancient opposition between the two men would peak, locking them into a kind of paralysis. They would begin to see that as long as the conflict between them persisted, they stood no chance of overcoming their common foe. It's then that they would commit to an exploration of their legacies in a most revealing and liberating manner: they would engage in a kiva ritual beyond the known. Guided by the spiritual ancestors of the ancient Anasazi people, these half-brothers of history would, out of shared adversity and great hunger for the truth, spend tortuous days and nights bringing their subterranean judgments and feelings into the light. Eventually, they each would claim it all, even the hate, as their own. They would track their legacies back through history, back to Abraham, the common father of their peoples, back to when we agreed to divide the spiritual and the material into opposition. They would see that in the rapid darkening of a world blindly following the old order, there was nothing for them to do but step completely into the new order. Anything short of total surrender to the new would spell disaster for themselves, their families, and humanity. They would commit to applying the long-hidden principle they had studied at their mystery school to create the foundation for a new order. This healing, and with it the men's acknowledgement that they are interdependent and are therefore harmonious aspects of a greater whole, would begin to catalyze a worldwide turnaround. By employing the principle at every turn, the veils would continue to fall.

Until this journey, the men would have seen themselves as functionaries for a unique healing work. Now, the work was no longer a form of therapy to be performed on others; it was unconditionally stepping into a new paradigm as a foundation for life. The time had come for people to actually walk across the bridge. It was not going to happen from without, through a leader or some unthinkable cataclysm; the choice belonged to humanity.

The men and their wives would next explore the historic relationship of man and woman from an energetic viewpoint, instead of as fear-based prisons of ideas called "isms." Each couple would discover the same hidden split that existed between the men. They would see how it guided their roles and relationships, and with the seeing, they would release all sources of friction and move to a viewpoint of harmony and effortlessness.

Once the parents were secure in their new perspective, their relationships with their children would naturally metamorphose into fullness for all. Soon these families would possess the strength and inner security to confront the greatest darkness yet. They would pay attention to a now-growing collective inner knowing, a formidable intuition, in recognizing the next step on their journey.

At this point in the plot, I would bring in the Hopi people and their prophecy, especially the legendary stone tablets. The fictional families would be called to the Grand Canyon, to raft and kayak the Colorado River. It would be here, at the sacred Hopi origination site along the Little Colorado, that the children would discover the lost half of the stone tablets.

The adventure would ultimately dovetail in a climactic encounter on a desolate Hopi mesa, where our heroes would overcome their adversaries, now revealed as the Illuminati, by using their mastery of stepping into the void--becoming empty and then mirroring the negativity back to its source. The ultimate, unbreakable strength of these now-aligned families would be a unified energy field produced by releasing all opposition and harmonizing with the one meridian, the flow of energy that pulses through all life on this planet. At this final confrontation, the families would demonstrate their commitment to non-violence by effortlessly and fearlessly standing as a circle of consensus. The harder the Illuminati pushed, the further back they'd bounce, as if they were fighting a field of the absent-minded professor's flubber, ultimately failing in their mission to keep the tablets separate.

After the battle, the protagonists would return the lost half of the stone tablets to its home with the Hopi caretakers and to its matching tablet for the prophesied beginning of the next civilization. The contents of the now-restored tablet would reveal the very same principle of human beings' relationship to life on this planet that the men had studied at the mystery school. That school would have been in keeping with the fabled schools from a now-lost past, where the true seekers were taught the deepest principles of life, then kept the candles burning while the rest of the world plunged ever deeper into the whirlpools of materiality.

Finally, since the Illuminati were the sinister, secret society appointed to keep the material-scientific civilization on course, its defeat would mean the conclusion of this epoch.

At dawn on December 25, 2011, our heroes silently stand together with the Hopi elders on the mesa, looking out over the ruins of this civilization. They welcome the future with great joy.

The End.

The fantasy would serve as entertainment and a parable to boot. The idea germinated about the time I was getting divorced. It served to keep alive my dreams about family, the future, and parent-child transmissions, once the burned-out shell of family became my reality.

At the same time, I began to give acupuncture treatments to a woman who had also attended my acupuncture school. She was first and foremost a student of the long-hidden Life Principle of Kototama, literally, "the word soul." One day, I told her about the concept for my novel. She replied that fiction was a lie.

"If you are addressing the Life Principle, then tell the truth," she simply concluded.

Fiction arises largely from emotion, inspiration, and imagination, which are, according to the work I do, only three of five aspects of the spiritual dimension. And, the spiritual dimension is only one of five dimensions that human beings have available to fully manifest who we are on this planet. Therefore, each moment of reality is composed of so much more.

But, I reasoned, everyday life is so repetitive, usually boring compared to my rarefied storyline. How could truth be engaging? How could it compete with a metaphysical thriller? As I wondered, I plunged into an ever-deepening process of transformation. The divorce had sprung me from a dream existence into a riveting world of feelings. The more I allowed myself to feel the suffering, the hungrier I grew to apply my Life Medicine education to releasing the delusion that had created my pain. Instead of concentrating on healing others, my focus shifted to my own limitations. Whenever I got stuck, the right tools appeared. So too, did helpers from the spirit realm. With the search, I forgot about my dilemma around fact or fiction. Reality and the truth of each moment became my arena, and awakening fully to it became my primary desire. I discovered that the awakening process does not need to be drama-driven or filled with violence to be captivating.

One day, I set to the writing, and the form--personal essay--effortlessly revealed itself. I grasped that the exotic fantasy holds limits for the reader when it comes to matters of transformation. Real-life tales are more accessible in the most vibratory sense of the word.

Many years ago, before my medical career, I was a writer. Everything I wrote sold. Then, one day as I was sitting in my study, I ran into a wall. I knew I needed to discover and then practice my life's work before I could resume writing. I stopped that very day and did not look back until twelve years later, when the novel idea began to germinate.

During that period, I actually did attend a mystery school, where I received my primary tool for exploration: the Life Principal of Kototama. The school existed for a only short while, and I was privileged to be there at the heart of the teaching. It was purportedly an acupuncture college, but this was simply a tag used to legitimize a much greater teaching. After the first two classes had completed their basic studies, the new students began clamoring for more acupuncture teaching and began to resent my teacher's primary dedication to the Life Principle. They could not see that by applying the Life Principal to Oriental Medicine, he had transformed the medicine, moving it out of the present civilization and into the next. Their resistance was excruciating for him to confront; he was encountering the reality of a still-peaking material-scientific civilization.

A peerless teacher, Sensei M. Nakazono's own teachers came from a profound array of the greatest healers, intellectuals, martial artists, and mystics in the world. He succeeded in bringing the Life Principle back into society, and foresaw his students crossing the bridge into the new civilization.

The Life Principle was hidden thousands of years ago, when we human beings collectively agreed to dramatically shift direction in consciousness and to explore the realm of the physical senses. Our desire to follow what felt good overrode our knowing of what such a course ultimately would become: a road of separation and violence. The word "agreed" is central here. A-greed became our motive vibration, since the desires connected to the material realm are of an insatiable nature. When proceeding from this viewpoint, we can never get enough.

Having developed the capacity to destroy all life on this planet, we are reaching the end of this four-fold way of seeing. The path of materiality, according to the Life Principle, is held in place unconsciously by a specific vibratory relationship of fifty sounds. These sound vibrations create up all material reality.

Sensei M. Nakazono told my class how Japan was propelled into World War II by the new Shinto religion, which was based on the material-scientific order of the fifty sounds. Even today, Japanese schoolchildren daily recite the fifty sounds in this sequence, as their alphabet.

Lest we judge Japan too quickly, he also discussed America's destiny, as reflected by the fifty stars in our flag. The stars symbolize the night we have walked through these thousands of years pursuing the material-scientific way. It is in the United States where this civilization is culminating. Sensei was emphatic that there would never be a 51st state.

When our ancestors decided to follow the material-scientific path, they agreed to hide the Life Principle. We could not have fully developed the material-scientific civilization, nor its accompanying artistic-religious civilization, while remaining conscious of the Life Principle. The principle was held and passed from generation to generation by a small circle of people. Many of those people died protecting it.

The Life Principle is also based on the fifty sound vibrations, but in this paradigm, the order of the sounds is different; the relationship of the human being to the world is quite simply restored to right-side-up. What is our individual responsibility becomes clear.

The Life Principle is a tool, which, when applied appropriately, has nothing to do with dogma or ideas. The principle is reflected everywhere within the body of this book; for readers desiring a more specific discussion, I have included a short appendix. My exploration of the principle has been that of a student and remains so.

The stories you'll read here, with the exception of the prelude, are a collection of essays that I wrote between August of 1992 and November of 1994. They have confluences that merge to form one story, appearances at times to the contrary. The synergy of the book is best experienced by reading the stories from front to back, rather than at random.

I believe that we stand at the frontier of a new mythology as we enter the final years of this millennium, and I see storytelling as the creation vehicle for that mythology. The stories in this volume reveal the emergence of a new order, one that is awakening within us all, if we so choose.

Only now, having lived these stories, has the fictional version--my original novel--revealed itself to me in its entirety. And now, more than ever, I feel delighted that I chose to tell the real story. After all, the time has come to return home.

Prelude

Wake of Thanksgiving, 1990. Oh, my little boy, my little boy. He hurts so bad, feels so trapped. Betrayed, abandoned by God. I stand, a man, frozen, prisoner to my fears. I have, therefore, nothing to give him; I protect my heart just as he protects his. In the deep of the night our souls reach for one another, pleading to be full, free from this numbing slow death passage. Having held him close for hours, I gently lift him and move him over; he lets out an angry scream of "No" while remaining asleep.

Earlier today he went back to his mother's home, and now I rage that there is nowhere to go, that nothing matters, and that change and the journey are only illusions. I speak of other worlds, but I am dying the death of my ancestors.

He was born a warrior. I was born aloof. Late last summer, he gave me his teddy bear to keep me company when I realized that he wouldn't be living with me. Today, it ended up with him again, somehow. What will fill that space?

My heart tightens, breathing grows labored as night falls. I am alone. He is alone.

Yesterday, at first light, I saw two deer, a mother and a doe, moving through the yard, seeking the last of autumn's harvest. And what else, I wondered, went on between them?

This morning, while I am running, a stag appears, in full antler headress. He approaches me casually, not the least bit apprehensive, and crosses the trail directly in front of me. I feel the pain of his solitude, but he wears it as a part of his fullness. Then he is gone. The scent of dignity remains.

Emergencies and States of Mind

"I'm so afraid. I think I'm dying."

I had vowed there would be no deaths on my shift, and here I was, trapped in an elevator in complete darkness with a dying man.

He was elderly and had already undergone four heart surgeries. I was young, supporting my family by working as an Emergency Medical Technician at this innovative health care center.

I shouted for help, but received no answer. I imagined the other staff members in the new building, now without power, had their own crises to contend with. In the silence, I could hear the old man's heartbeats grow louder, so I took a few breaths and moved toward him.

I dug deep into some intuitive recess for the answer, propelled by his repeated cries that he was dying. I instructed him, breath by precious breath, in relaxed breathing while my hands led me to various points on his body, where I applied touch, not pressure.

Slowly, through that endless darkness, I repeated the breathing instructions and followed my hands, and slowly, ever so slowly, his heartbeats ceased to echo off the walls. Only after he was stable did I hear calls coming down the elevator shaft. They had found us, and the auxiliary generator was about to come on.

The experience inspired me to double my intention for there to be no deaths or even deep traumas while I was on duty. For 36 hours each week I worked at the center, sleeping beside a panel that responded to the pull of a "guest room" emergency cord.

The center was modeled after those designed by the late Nathan Pritikin. Guests would commit to a month-long stay, wherein they would eat a fat-free vegetarian diet and follow prescribed daily regimens using the underground indoor track, swimming pool, weight and exercise rooms, biofeedback facilities, outdoor track, and open space. Daily lectures emphasized the evils of tobacco, alcohol, and stress, and patients met regularly with their on-site physicians. And the place attracted some very sick people. Triple heart bypasses were common, as were multiple stroke sufferers.

My prior experience with emergency health care was not nearly so glamorous or plush. I had volunteered on an ambulance in the mountains of northern New Mexico, where I encountered gunshot and knife wounds. I hated seeing the violence that we commit on ourselves and each other, but I discovered a passion for working with people, and my sensitivity to the suffering of others, dormant since childhood, resurfaced on those rides.

That I had gravitated to health care at all was a complete surprise, since the aptitude/interest batteries that every American kid was subjected to never indicated doctor or nurse as my livelihood, let alone acupuncturist. My grandfather had singled me out to become a lawyer. But I had now been accepted to begin studies with a master acupuncture teacher, and soon I would take the next step toward my calling.

On my last working day at the center, I felt gratitude for the grace I had experienced while working there--no one had died under my care. I packed my belongings and began bidding farewell to people who had become my friends. About five minutes remained when suddenly the gardener came charging through the door to tell me that two semi trucks had collided head-on at the highway entrance to the center, a half-mile down the road. Kit in hand, I was off.

As I sped down the road, I heard sirens approaching. When I arrived, a policeman informed me that my services would not be needed. Both men had been decapitated.

Only weeks later, I was sitting zazen at my acupuncture college. When an ambulance siren would break our concentration, my teacher would gravely shake his head and say, "Not necessary." To him, the siren signaled that life was being lived out of balance, that someone had chosen to violate natural law.   My path was just beginning.

Till Death Do . . .

Lisa reached the outside door of my acupuncture office, supported step by step by her husband Rick. Framed in late autumn twilight, she turned back to face me and the office staff, and broke into an all-is-well, other-worldly grin.

"It's been real," was all she said.

Those were the last words I would hear her speak.

It was a Friday, only a week past her twenty-eighth birthday. Two days later, there was a power outage all over town, and she and Rick had a peaceful, candlelit time together, free from electrical interference, before he had to make the ten-hour drive back to their home and to his teaching job at the college.

The next morning I received a call from Lisa's live-in housekeeper informing me that in the night Lisa had gone into a coma. I canceled my treatments and went to her apartment, wanting to help, but knowing better. Three days later, per her instructions, her body was cremated.

Afterwards, family and friends gathered to remember. Rick showed slides while recounting their adventuring life together. The light on the wall revealed a beautiful couple searching the wild places, questing for shared purpose, propelled by the fire of a young love: a coast-to-coast motorcycle tour on one motorcycle, mountain biking, backpacking, setting up home in rural west Texas. They laughed, they took risks, yet their vision for a life together ultimately fell into fragments. They allied only in extreme politics, the language of "us" and "them." They began to drift apart.

From the depths of their separation came the joint desire to reunite, and they chose a wilderness setting for their journey--a kayak trip through the Big Bend. The trip revealed that at the root their love was still alive.

On the last day out, Lisa overturned in a rapids and took a long swim in frigid water. When her pneumonia worsened, hospitalization revealed cancer raging unabated through her liver and lungs. The prognosis was for a turbulent, quick death. Within minutes, Rick was calling my office, since I had treated one of their best friends from college, who had also had cancer and had experienced a full recovery.

I told them to come up but made no promises. As I diagnosed Lisa for the first time, her friends held vigil in the waiting room. My primary tool for diagnosis is pulse reading, with six pulses on each wrist, plus an additional pulse that reveals a person's life will. If the life will pulse is in a certain condition, the individual will die soon, even if she is symptom free.

Lisa's life will pulse felt fine, but her other twelve pulses--relating to the flow of life energy through the body and to the vital synchronization of expanding and contracting energy--tetered on the edge of possible repair. They sounded like an orchestra without a conductor, without consensus, splintering further away from harmony with each heartbeat. After telling Lisa and Rick my diagnosis, we agreed to give it a go.

They secured an apartment that day, and I drew up a strict healing diet, which Lisa unhesitatingly embraced. Rick promised to visit each weekend.

At one of her first treatments, she recalled, out of the blue, an incident from the previous summer, on a night when she and Rick were camping in the sagebrush country of Wyoming.

"We were sitting by the campfire when I saw an owl fly up from the only tree around. It circled directly above us in three counterclockwise circles, fluttering and making noises as if speaking to us, alighted on the tree, and then repeated the act three more times, before disappearing into the night. When the owl was gone I wept long and hard and couldn't understand why."

I fell silent, having recognized the nature of this omen from Native American stories.

She looked directly at me and said, "You know what that meant, don't you?"

I nodded, and she revealed that she, too, knew this had been the harbinger of her death.

"It could mean a spiritual death," I remarked, but without saying so, we both felt otherwise.

For several weeks, Lisa functioned normally, needing only lots of rest. But after another month, she was bedridden, twenty pounds lighter, and wan from head to toe. One of her good friends became her housekeeper, and from that point on, I made housecalls for treatments.

By the day, I watched a miracle happen. The weaker she became, the more unconditional she grew toward life. Her defiant smile softened, and she became radiant. There was no self-pity, only wonder at the "opportunity" that she had been given. She did not have the energy to talk much, but her presence conveyed it all: Lisa was realizing what she had come for. The simple barrio apartment began to feel like a temple.

As her physical condition continued to deteriorate, she had only gratitude for me, while I struggled to find the answer, the miracle combination of points that would make her well. I would frequently lapse into self-pity around "my failure."

Thanksgiving came and with it, Lisa's birthday. She began to get stronger, to show signs of a turnaround. Everyone felt celebratory. As the surge continued, she decided to return to my office for her treatments.

I stood proud on her first day back, joining in the giddiness that accompanied her into the treatment room, until, that is, I felt her pulses. The form of acupuncture I practice is called Life Medicine. A major tenet of this medicine stipulates that if a person's life will pulse is gone, then I cannot continue to help this individual, and must therefore stop the treatments.

I looked at Lisa, and she returned a knowing, loving smile. I looked at Rick and saw that he did not yet consciously know. I violated protocol that afternoon and treated her, acting as if all was well. She returned to the waiting room, still filled with the giddiness of her friends and loved ones, as day gave way to night.

A week later, Rick carried her ashes to the desert canyon country of Utah and spread them over the quiet, red earth.

A Gift Bringer

Even over the phone, I could feel his charisma and his importance, but beyond these, I sensed that a gift bringer was coming my way. This in a time when the wise ones have gone silent, or have been absent, ignored, or overlooked.

I was midway through my second year of acupuncture college when he called me for a consultation. We had converted the master bedroom of our old adobe into a treatment room to accommodate my growing patient load. Technically, I was in over my head, but who was I to question the parade of Mercedes that arrived those afternoons on our dirt road?

Upon our meeting, his persona turned out to be even more impressive: he carried a great shock of white, curly hair, to complement deep, dark, wild eyes and a boyish grin. He was constantly stalking, not one to waste words, so we got down to business right away.

I felt nervous to be in the role of healer with this man, but he sunk quickly into trusting receptivity. At treatment's end, he asked me how long I had been doing this work, and I responded that I was still in school.

"No," he said, "I mean how many lifetimes have you been a healer?"

The words touched my core. I felt myself being called out, recognized as I never had been. And with those words, my destiny became clear.

He became the focal point for a kind of magical unfoldment. Although our talk was limited, I held what was spoken as sacred. He revealed to me the specific mountains where Santa Fe's spiritual center lies, and from that time on, my runs would carry me to those places, where I would always stop to give thanks to the ancestors and to meditate.

He told me how he never thought he could live anywhere but Santa Fe until he was yanked away by World War II. He knew without my saying so that I held the city in the same light as he had, in a passionate, seemingly insatiable embrace.

"But the war did show me that I could live happily elsewhere," he assured me, "and I have been a freer man ever since."

He saw my future, he recognized my weaknesses, and from these, he offered me his truth: "You have a long race to run, Stuart. Don't push yourself too hard now, even though your energy feels boundless, because you will pay later if you override."

But I am no ordinary person governed by regular laws, I thought, as he spoke. When he saw that my head had already begun to swell, he did not warn me again.

His wisdom emerged as if from a spring. And he addressed truths that I would often not grasp for years. For example, he urged me to consider that my wife and I having intercourse without protection would be a vital ingredient in bringing us to our deepest intimacy.

"I can't stress how important this will be to your relationship over time, Stuart. How you decide to do this will be up to the two of you."

Although he had children of his own and I had parents of my own, I was coming to embrace this eccentric man with the sparkling eyes, this nervous genius, as one of my select circle of elders.

Our treatments were proceeding very well until one afternoon, when he arrived appearing exhausted and traumatized. He explained that he had taken a long hike the day before, as was one of his customary passions, this time to an ancient and still active Pueblo Indian shrine. He had felt great negotiating the six miles of steep canyons and high mesas on the way in, but upon arriving, he explained, "I suddenly felt all of my life energy being drawn out of me by the shrine." The trek back was pure survival, climaxing in a virtual crawl in the darkness toward the trail's end and the safety of his car.

I cannot say that I ever saw his vitality return fully after that day. Soon thereafter, I launched into a full-time practice, and we stopped meeting regularly. Without realizing it, I was now on my own.

One of our last encounters took me by surprise. At that time, I was peaking, feeling quite full of myself in regard to my healing capacity; in retrospect, I was a disaster in the making. It was an exquisite autumn afternoon and I had just finished a treatment and was heading out to the waiting room to greet my next patient, when he burst unannounced into my treatment room.

He was irritated, on the offensive, in my face, and standing in my domain.

"I understand that you are treating people with AIDS," he charged.

The sweep of the epidemic was just then beginning to register on the national psyche, and fear of contagion was rising fast. Use of disposable needles had not yet become standard procedure in my profession. True, I was considering treating people carrying the virus because I desired the challenge, but to my knowledge I was not treating anyone who was HIV-positive.

Looking back, I believe that he sensed my self-destruction in progress and came to slap me back to my senses.

When I denied that I was treating anyone with AIDS, he told me not to do it, ever, then turned abruptly and vanished as quickly as he had appeared.

And so the lessons came, ones I had to experience, and eventually I felt myself pushing against a wall of my own creation. I was already midstream in a malpractice suit, and by year's end my marriage would lay in ruins. My motive vibration had become terror and anxiety, a life of reaction. Yet a recent kayak trip down a challenging river revealed that I was at the peak of my physical power.

From a faraway place inside me, a voice told me that the time had come for a vision quest, and that I must journey to the very shrine where the old man had almost died.

I prepared for the quest by sitting in hot springs at a Zen monastery for several days, quieting my mind, not talking with another human being, until I felt ready. Then, on a Sunday morning in early April, I ventured out.

I negotiated rushing streams and a recently-thawed trail on that brilliant day, feeling stronger with every step. As I reflected on my son's upcoming birthday and how I had promised to get him his first knife, I reached a creek and leapt across. In motion, my eyes caught sight of an object lying on a boulder. The exact model of Swiss army knife my son wanted was now in my hands. In my exuberance, I called upstream and down for its possible owner, hoping to not be answered. Only silence greeted me.

Finding the knife was a kind of cosmic response to a commitment I made just before the quest. My family had suffered during the years that I strove to perfect my healing skills. I obsessively poured my vital energy, even the dreamtime, into grasping the medicine. During those days of vision quest preparation at the monastery, I clarified my intention to take a more active, more alive role in parenting. The knife served notice that my return trip had begun.

I walked on, gazing out at still-snowy peaks to the east and to the west, bouyed by the omen of change, ready to meet the shrine. Soon, obsidian, eagle feathers, deer antlers, and many other simple objects greeted me. I had arrived. In the distance, Indian drums were beating.

Once again, my eyes were taken, this time to a nearby field, where I observed three depressions of land, all about the same size. I realized that I had just discovered three unexcavated ceremonial kivas, places where the ancestors had journeyed underground into the darkness, sometimes for months, to face their inner demons.

With the discovery came the truth: I was numb, I was dying. Before I could ever consider ascending into the enlightened realms, I must journey down into my personal kiva, the realm of my feelings. The vision I was questing for came in a flash.

I began my walk back, knowing that the ice was breaking, escorted by a single raven. I had wandered through my adult life trying to rise above my pain as well as the rest of my feelings. The vision made it clear that the time had come for me to confront those feelings. I felt grateful. I tasted trepidation, and I savored it. I felt the onset of an irreversible tide of sweeping change.

As I neared the trail's end at twilight, I wondered what the elder had come for that day. I could not figure it out. All I saw was his contagious smile. Suddenly I realized that it surfaced from a sea of feelings. Then and there, I grasped that his transmission to me was complete.

Return to Atalaya

We were a perfect match--Santa Fe and I--during that period of my life. Perhaps it was the only town in the country that could hold the intensity of what I was to experience there; perhaps it provoked that intensity.

The first message that the city would someday be my home arrived during a walk along its Cathedral Place with my then-wife and Laibrook, our two-year-old son. It was a lovely evening: springtime had securely taken its soft hold, at 7,000 feet, in the sky city. I heard a voice then: "You have lived here before and you will again, to complete unfinished business."

What joy I felt. Since we had moved to a small village in northern New Mexico six months previous, I had been increasingly drawn to Santa Fe, seeking any excuse, any reason to be there, to walk the ancient winding roads, to savor the brilliant play of shadow and

light, to discover hidden courtyards, to listen to chamber
music, to touch the endless adobe walls and to feel them
breathe, to explore the mountains and high desert, to
luxuriate in the cafes. I had fallen hard, for a place, and
I could not stay away.

What a surprise, since on first impression, some
years before, I perceived a town filled with aloof and
arrogant artists and artist-types, and was told that the
mountains were filled with rattlesnakes. I have since
come to revere first impressions as saints of mine, but I
am a Leo with a full moon in Pisces, and romance is my
middle name.

We were a young family, and I moved awkwardly
with it. As far as making a living was concerned, I
sought to keep the magic alive that I had known while
instructing wilderness-as-therapy programs. But I no
longer felt at ease with working away from home as a
way of life, and, being an uncompromising sort, I was
awaiting my new calling that spring night on Cathedral
Place.

Eighteen months and some extraordinary synchronicity and great trials and tribulations later, we were packed
and on our way to the "city different." As our moving
caravan rolled onto the dirt road on the old east side, I
cried the tears of a man coming home after an infinitude.
My wife cried the tears of being pulled apart from her

family and of being exiled for an indefinite time to this half-foreign country.

The move occurred on Indian Market weekend, when the city swells to twice its size. A late summer rain had just freshened the air. We were greeted by our neighbors/landlords, an Hispanic couple in the deepest Santa Fe sense, and by the woman's elderly father, who lived in the compound. And by a rainbow stretching between two mountains that I would come to know very well. On this day, I became a part of one of those special places in time.

Across the road, goats grazed, and the scent of ponderosa, piñon, and juniper wafted down from the nearby mountains as we unloaded. I carried Kai, born on the total eclipse of the sun six months before, on my back in a baby pack. It would be in this manner that he and I would mostly convene over the next two years.

I was a man on a quest. I was of a singular laser vision, intending to dig deep for a pearl to pass on to my children, something for them to build a foundation on, something I felt certain that I would find in Santa Fe. No ordinary pearl: I was questing for essence. A world filled with dead ritual had spurred my search.

Whenever omens appeared that I did not like, I would deny them, or interpret them to my liking. For example, the day after I was accepted to study Life Medicine and was offered a teaching job that would support us, my wedding ring fell off and disappeared. I took this to mean that our marriage was moving to a higher, more spiritual--and therefore less material--level. Once my schooling was underway, my senior classmates told me that no marriage among them was surviving the changes the students were going through. My silent response was that we were different, that late each night over tea, I would tell her of what I had learned, because she and I were going together. And for the first two years, I did.

Each morning brought with it the sense of rebirth, of promises for possibilities beyond what was known. The light and the air were so clear, so fresh, so infinite. I was electric in my non-stop demeanor. I felt on top of the world, barely touching it, surging to capture it all. Awaken at five A.M., stretch and meditate. Then, grade papers and make lesson plans. Off to teach by eight. After school, I could usually bring one or both of my boys along for activities with the school's outdoor program that I ran, be it climbing, hiking, ropes course, or skiing. Then, a quick dinner, and I became a student for three hours, followed by tea at home. Weekends meant study groups with my classmates, outdoor program activities, time with my family. This was the first year, after which things only got busier, once I began to give treatments.

Despite the heavy schedule, I savored Santa Fe, and was determined to experience its every mood, in every nook and cranny, at every season. Afternoon bike rides with one of the boys on the back, at the peak of autumn. In the distance, the largest stands of aspen in the country smiled down on us, brilliant in yellow and orange, while I pedaled up Canyon Road, once a path to the mountains for firewood. The town would be empty, virtually free from tourists, luxurious in the warm air, looking so beautiful to me: the architecture, the gardens, the intriguing shops, galleries, and restaurants. I knew where the ripe fruit trees and berry patches lie, and soon, so did the boys. The people were gracious, generous to us. On brisk afternoons that welcomed the scent of piñon back into the air, we would play football with some of my students at a mystical park that felt like another world. Beer-drinking low riders would watch, but never bother us. Or, we would climb the steep ladders to an ancient ceremonial kiva and return along the sweet stream at dusk, under the full moon, when the native ones were just beginning their walk to maintain the shrines. Around every bend, magic lie in wait for me.

I was insatiable, exploring hidden plazas, dragging one of the boys along with me to listen to chamber music, attending a pueblo dance on a high mesa at winter dawn, discovering new trails, meeting the unique group of extraordinary souls who lived in Santa Fe. I learned, for instance, at which supermarket the eccentrics shopped and where the creme de la creme went for their groceries. These places became regular stops on weekends for me and the boys. Not for a moment, did I take life for granted. Rarefied, the place was so rarefied, that the grocery stores were utterly fascinating. As was the old Federal Building where I would meet special friends and, under stately trees, practice Tai Chi on the biggest lawn in town, while the winos observed. And those undulating mountain trails that would make for nice walks, if located anywhere else, took on spiritual significance, whether bathed in the deep white light of winter on exhilarating backcountry ski descents, or serving as guides on my pilgrimages to rare species of wildflower at midsummer. The ancestors would talk to me, on mountaintops and along trails that I kept returning to.

At center stage, however, lay my quest. From the opening ceremony, when my teacher told us that not one of us really knew why we had come, when he asked us to leave all that we thought we knew at the door, free for us to reclaim at the end of our studies, for four years, every class was absolutely captivating. I entered into a realm of study that was alive, breathing, challenging me as if I were kayaking or climbing on an extreme edge, where his every word reflected the vitality of the medicine that I studied, and where the only constant was change. I had never gone in for gurus; the principles that we were studying transcended one person, and yet, I felt privileged to be studying with a peerless teacher in his prime.

But the quest had a drive that became blinding, and in its flush, I dedicated myself to being successful, to becoming the best knight of all. I had relegated my search to a competition. I became driven, and in the intoxication, my head swelled. More treatments equated with being the best; likewise treating the rich and famous.

The one constant that my teacher had transmitted in every class, was the admonition, "You must suffer."

When my world fell apart, it manifested in a day, with a rush of pain and disorientation, that finally, finally conveyed to me what he had really meant. Then, there was nothing that I could do to push the pain away or to get my world back. I ran to the mountaintops, seeking guidance from the ancestors, but I was greeted with an aloof silence. At the mountains' feet, more and more new homes were pushing up and into these sacred realms, and there was nothing that I could do to stop them.

With the fall, came a greater need for friends, for intimacy. But most of the people I knew backed off, fearing that my pain was contagious, not liking to see me in that light. And my teacher had long since turned in a direction that I could not embrace.

The end of my time in Santa Fe was near, and the truth hit home about a year later, when I was guiding my now three boys down a nearby river. We were camped amidst robust ponderosa pine on a soft summer morning. Mikael, forever my baby, then seven, asked me to escort him into the woods to find a suitable spot to set up the toilet. We found a gem of a place, and I began to walk away and give him privacy, when, out of the corner of my eye, I saw it: a huge rattlesnake, coiled, not a foot from him. Call it grace, call it blindness, but not in thirteen years had I seen a rattlesnake anywhere in New Mexico.

When it is time to go, it's best to acknowledge the reality and to do it gracefully. Two months later, I observed the morning of my birthday by watching the sun rise directly over Sun Mountain, a sacred peak. From the front yard of what had been our family's home, it also came up in that same position months earlier, on my now-ex-wife's birthday. Every year, on those two days. At our home, we had shared an alignment with a sacred mountain, but not with each other. Curiously, she chose to remain in Santa Fe.

The next day, I was heading out of town with my new partner, in search of more healing and not clear of much beyond that. I was broken by a dream in ruins.

Late summer clouds had gathered and were now celebrating their release, as lightning filled the air in every direction. The negative ions made me feel alive. To the New Mexico border, the ride was pure magic, a light show to match any of the many I had witnessed in that extraordinary land. The more that it rained, the more I cried--tears of gratitude. Brilliant hues of blue and purple lit up the Rio Grande Gorge.

It was at the state line that I got it: from that moment on, no matter where I would be, Santa Fe was forever part of me, and my leaving was a gift, my freedom.

Pyramid Power

During my period of greatest self-importance in
Santa Fe, I called in a malpractice lawsuit. It made me
begin to question how I could accept my judgment ever
again, especially in the volatile and highly litiguous realm
of health care. So when I left Santa Fe, I stopped
practicing and moved further each day from any desire to
begin again, because I saw no solution to my self-doubt.
I finally decided to quit forever from practicing medicine
as I knew it.

Nine months later, I was in Mexico, sitting atop the
highest pyramid in the Yucatan, looking out over five
lakes and imagining an ancient network of fifty roads
that once emanated out from the city, when a voice from
deep within told me that the Life Principle, as I understood it, would be a primary tool for moving our world

into the new civilization. The voice, I was told, was of the Mayan ancestors.

I was stunned. For years, I had felt that I was on a mission, and that it was about my healing work, but since quitting my practice, I had neither intention nor desire to start again. Besides, the notion of my mission had gone sour, and I now identified it with more violent sacrifice, as going like soup and sandwich with the current of the material-scientific civilization. My mission now held nothing for me besides suffering, separation, heartbreak, and disillusionment. For me, it represented a time of deep loneliness, increasing alienation from my children, divorce, and feeling ultimately more alone in the world than when I began.

So what had I just heard? When my partner and I descended from the pyramid, I felt altered, lighter, and we returned along a trail now bright with the greatest profusion of tropical butterflies I have ever seen.

We drove back to our tent on the ocean, and she asked me to treat her, as she had begun to feel ill. I still carry my little blue needle bag wherever I travel, but on this occasion, I did not open it. I found myself using my hands in place of needles, and the results were astonishing. My partner said it was the best treatment I had ever given her, and, for my part, during the treatment, I constantly felt in contact with her essence. I had been standing in "naka-ima," the here and now. I

had felt clear, attentive, and free from ego. My directive
for the treatment was pure and intuitive. There was no
separation between practitioner and patient, as there is
with needles, wherein the practitioner turns the treatment
over to the needles and speculates at a distance on
appropriate dosage instead of feeling the process with
hands on, moment to moment, and clearly discerning the
time when the patient arrives at the balance. Because I
had been in touch with her every feeling, I was believing
in myself and the process. Truth is of the moment, it
being a direct reflection of reality, and the vantage point
that I had just held left no room for anything but the
collective truth. There had been no opportunity for my
self-importance to take over the treatment with its
cleverness and its insatiability for outside approval. I
had stood in the realm of consensus, a place where I was
as vulnerable as my patient, a place where we witnessed
our truth. There was nothing for me to do in this space
but to be myself. Now here was a situation where I
could believe myself, beyond any doubt. The treatment
had filled me with wonder, and I could not ask for more.

Without needles, which puncture and are a form of
surgery, I was now working in a non-violent realm,
which meant less fear and therefore less contraction. In
this context, I could more easily hold up the life mirror
as a direct reflection of the person I was treating. I had
discovered a way in which the course of treatment was

effortlessly transmitted to me, where the source of imbalance was revealed, not speculatively, but from the collective empty space, a place that constantly exists beyond our phenomonal grasp. My job was simply to facilitate the transmission.

That day in the Yucatan, my life's work began.

Leander

August 9, 1992. 11 A.M. Forty-seven years ago, at this very moment, the bomb descended on Nagasaki. In Santa Fe, New Mexico, my former home, and only miles as the crow flies from where the bomb was conceived, a memorial service for a boy I knew is in progress.

Leander plunged to his death eight days ago from near the summit of 14,000-foot Mount Sneffels, in Colorado's San Juan range. He and my son Kai were classmates at a private elementary school. His father, Preston, and I kayaked a river together last spring, and we had originally planned to be with all of our boys on a river trip at the very time of Leander's fall.

Several of the people who will be attending the service told me that Leander was preparing for his death, that it was no accident. After he died, magic entered the lives of the circle he had touched: Birds flew into homes; Leander's books appeared in classmate's bedrooms; friends wrote stories, as if from nowhere, and wanted to give them to Leander, all the while not knowing that he was gone.

The service is being held under a giant tent where a reportedly enlightened soul from India arrives each summer to bless all who come to see her. I am told that with Leander's death has risen an outpouring of honesty and love, the likes of which no one there has known.

When the river trip with Preston and Leander fell through (my boys were not hungry to go, and I had grown sick of pushing them), Leander told his dad that he wanted to visit people and places from his early childhood in Colorado. They did run a river, during which Leander put on a headlamp one night and went to work drawing exotic symbols until morning by applying mud to a sandstone canyon wall, just as Carl Jung had spent his final days.

Then Leander asked if they could try Sneffels again, since they had failed to gain the peak on an earlier attempt. Preston agreed. While visiting Ouray, they unexpectedly ran into a classmate of Leander's, and he and his family joined Preston and Leander for the climb.

Once on the summit, Preston discovered his camera had one shot left, so he asked his companions to take a picture of him and Leander. Then the two boys started their descent.

Suddenly Leander changed course, saying, "This is the way I always go down."

How could this be possible since this was the first time he had ever reached the top?

It was over in an instant, as scree turned to ice. His father carried him off the mountain in his arms.

When I scratched my plans for the river, I chose to go into the wilderness to explore relationship, to do a healing diet, and to claim my emotional body, to bring it out of deep freeze. To this end my partner and I travelled to the mountains.

The time was ripe for breakthrough: according to the ancient Mayan calendar, the period from July 22 through July 26 was a time when the past 520 years would fold back upon itself in a Moebius strip, a figure eight, thereby allowing us to free ourselves from that past. A veritable karmic release, if the intention was clear. Twice a day, I ate a small bowl of brown rice and seaweed, 120 grains to a bite, more or less, chewing to a liquid consistency.

Out among the mountains of Colorado, I declared my intention to release competition from my life, to release my desire to be a star, to release my inflated self-importance, to release jealousy, to release my picture of being a parent, to release any and all personas I had created, to release my lifelong stance as a victim, to release a life of reaction to phenomena. The exhaustion of a life lived in opposition manifested in long and deep sleeps. Slowly, I made contact with long-repressed emotions, especially my rage.

On the final day of the diet I found myself sleeping in the shadow of Mount Sneffels. The next morning I was drawn to the top of the highest hill in the vicinity. I sat in the hot sun, surrounded by stands of decaying junipers, flies swarming on and around me, meditating on Mount Sneffels. I was transfixed. The day before I had seen a funeral in progress along the Colorado mountain highway, and now my inner voice told me that I was having a death.

The next evening, after a day of testing my newfound sense of boundaries back in civilization, my stomach began convulsing in extreme pain. I felt that I was dying. My companion, an expert at catharsis, explained that my stomach was my feeling body telling me something, and that I was obliged to listen. Slowly what emerged were the feelings I had stuffed over a lifetime, in the name of control, in the name of survival, as a judgment legacy concerning which feelings are bad. She had warned me for months that I was sitting on a powder keg and that for me to be truly free, I would need to emotionally express and release these imprisoned feelings from my core.

The diet served to set the stage, to open the box. Through that night of excruciating pain, I saw myself as a miserable, twisted, contracted, little old man who had been squeezing the emotional life right out of himself. As my rage at myself intensified, I yelled and screamed and made many strange and unfamiliar sounds, slowly exorcising the little old man. At times during the process, I almost vomited. At the end of it, spent and free of pain, I was able to breathe more deeply and more fully into my belly than anytime in memory.

We spent the next two days resting in high alpine meadows and sitting in natural hot springs. On August 1, we began the drive home. As we left Ouray, several volunteer search and rescue vehicles screamed past us.

Upon arriving home, I heard the news about Leander via telephone from an old friend in Santa Fe. I exploded in grief, not surprise. What stirred me most was my love for Preston, a gifted teacher and craftsman, an exquisitely sensitive man, who only recently declared himself finally healed from the death of his first wife, Leander's mother, so many years before. Now he had lost his only child.

The last time I saw this special boy was on a class camping trip at the end of his and Kai's fourth-grade year. The children in that class were one of those rare magical groups that gather in purported randomness but whose synergy is in the name of destiny. They carried a contagious innocence into life, marked by a love of nature and of wonder. They also held an alchemy that transformed the ordinary into the enchanting.

Leander was by far the most serious of the group, perhaps reflecting the early loss of his mother. His father once told me that Leander held great trepidation about growing up. On camping trips, he would usually pair off with one friend in an intense one-to-one encounter for the entire trip. He had a speech impediment, which may have kept him apart from the larger group.

I joined the class for every wilderness trip they took over a three-year period, partly because they mesmerized me and partly to treat Kai for a childhood asthma condition. By the last trip, Kai was breaking through his asthma and had left my tent to be with his buddies. Conversation into the night from the boys' tents told me that their innocence was ending. A month later my divorce was final, and Kai became adamant about transferring to public school.

After the divorce, I moved to another city and lived apart from some or all of my children. When I could no longer stand it, I demanded that all the boys spend the school year with me.

One year ago today, I was moving into this house, readying it as the base for my first foray into full-time

single parenting. I knew on that day that it would be an
exercise in survival as a single parent and that I would
eventually break. But I was desperate, and I was out of
touch with the truth that my feelings revealed. Instead, I
invoked my ancestors' legacy and became my children's
servant. So break I did, which made me hunger for the
work I have done this summer. Now, I no longer feel
desperate.

When I called Kai to tell him the news, alongside
shock and grief, he found relief in the idea that Leander
had been preparing for his death.

"It's really wierd, Dad, that Leander's birthday
would have been in a few days," he told me. Leander's
thirteenth birthday.

I urged Kai to have his feelings, all of them.

When I lived in Santa Fe, I kept my feelings out of
my life. A far cry from today, when I feel my energy on
an edge. There's lots of it, with an almost poison
quality, a lifetime of stagnated feelings now on the
move. On the other side of the edge is a sense of being
born, of moving into a life apart from the narrow
systems I have always known, a feeling of freedom.
Once I fully release my rage I see that it is me who I am
angry with--every time. These are wake-up calls that
show me what I had agreed to in life. After I identify
such an agreement, I am free to release it.

Since the night of my emotional breakthrough, I desire a rebirth in my relationship with my boys. I want it alive every moment. It's all we have.

Father, Meet Son

My oldest son was 16 when we first met. Today, we stand shoulder to shoulder on the porch of his second-story apartment, which is jammed with people. I am here to celebrate Aaron's twenty-first birthday.

The school year has just begun, and the evening air on this Saturday speaks to that season where summer surrenders to autumn. We drink beer together for the first time ever and find ourselves laughing and shouting over the din of the party.

Friends, those souls whom he takes most seriously, continually arrive to pay the big guy their respects. I watch them first search inside, then spot us through the glass doors, and press toward us. I say "us" because tonight we are inseparable, an item of sorts, held together by some force that tells me that this is our coming out party. I am twice the age of everyone here, but I feel happy and at ease.

Aaron phoned earlier in the day to make sure that I was coming. I also sensed that he was calling to check up on me, since my relationship life of late has been particularly unsettled, and I have been feeling curiously detached from pretty much everything.

I began this day with a technical climb. The atmosphere carried a strange haze, and I experienced an unusual degree of fear on the climb. My field of vision was narrow; I felt contracted, unable to fully extend, to relax, or to flow on the rock. Also, my usually injury-free body was reflecting some slow-to-heal hurts, prompting me to end the climb short of the summit, something I'd never done before. I was feeling old.

Once home, I showered, downed some homeopathic extract for pain relief, took a nap, and upon awakening attempted to resolve my love life in a lengthy long-distance phone conversation. That failed, I grabbed a quick deli dinner at a slick natural food market. As I chewed, I pondered Aaron's birthday gift.

What mattered most to me was the card, or what I said on the card. He had spent the summer in Alaska with friends, working in a fish canning factory and exploring the wild country. This was only the most recent indication of his impulse to open his life up, to take risks, to honor his desire to discover unusual people and places.

I would write about that change in him and also comment on an event he recently conveyed to me: Upon his return from Alaska, he visited his folks in California. He was sitting in their living room one afternoon when an empty glass on an end table next to him suddenly shattered without any apparent reason.

This was the first concern he related to me when he returned last week. He could not understand it. He knew that he had not consciously done anything to make the glass shatter, but he could not separate himself from the event. He felt that I had the answer, perhaps from my experience with energy after practicing acupuncture for thirteen years.

In the card, I explained to him that the incident had to do with his *being* and that the tools to channel that energy were his inheritance. If he desired to grasp what had happened and to learn how to harness the energy, at the appropriate time the knowledge would be transmitted. I felt pleased with what I wrote and looked for a set of Norse oracle Runes to give him, but the store was sold out.

Now that I'm at his party, conversation with his friends reveals that what he would really like are a couple of Big Dog T-shirts. He introduces me to those I do not know as "my dad," and I get goose bumps in return.

They also tell me that Aaron has opened up and is much happier since I came into his life. Several of them actually thank me. With this revelation, a weight I carried all these years drops away.

The music cranks up another notch. A fourth keg is almost finished. We go inside to see Aaron receive his birthday cakes. Both cakes are outrageous, and the lewd one ends up in his face. He tells me he's been getting wild lately. I tell him that I once passed out in this very apartment.

It is past ten, so we hug goodnight and I walk out, reflecting that now we are, we simply are. I look back and notice one young man hanging by a hand from the porch. Our becoming is fun.

Mom's Eyes

These days when I look at Mom, her eyes look softer, happier than I can remember them. Her posture continues to improve and her energy more resembles the dynamo from my youth than her post-operative cancer shadow of seven years ago.

She is a wonder, yet as her birthday approaches, she is increasingly in the grip of a titanic struggle. On that day her driver's license will expire, and with it will most likely go her freedom to drive. Behind those eyes, her retinas have been deteriorating, and her vision is failing. She is petrified.

Hers has been a life of selflessness, an expression of giving that embraces martyrdom as a way of life. Mom was the middle child, one of three girls, the daughter of an overweight and chronically-depressed mother and a Jewish immigrant father from Poland who boarded the boat by himself at age twelve, the day before World War I ignited.

He became a tailor who gave his all to his family's existence during America's lean times. Mom remembers Sunday drives, pleasure outings, where she could only imagine the scenery because my grandfather had the car windows plastered with ads for his business.

It was on one of those drives, when she was three years old, that the back door flew open as her father turned a corner, and she rolled out onto the street. Only her older sister Evy saw it happen. When Evy told her parents that my mother had fallen out of the car, my grandmother fainted, prompting Grandpa Morris to find the nearest drugstore.

"The druggist ran out with smelling salts and revived Grandma, while I continued to wait in the middle of the street," Mom recalls. "Fortunately, there was very little traffic in those days. They never took me to a doctor or anything. I think they got so excited about Grandma that they forgot about me."

She barely had time to catch her breath when her baby sister arrived. In short order, Mom was changing Janice's diapers, fixing her bottles, and saying an abrupt goodbye to childhood. By the time she was in high school, she was working at a five-and-dime store on weekends and raising Janice the rest of the time. When she talks about those days, she turns animated only when she recalls her high school acting experiences, but silently dismisses them as something that could never have continued.

During my childhood, I remember a woman who always showed up, but with shoulders bent and head bowed. Her most common utterance then, as now, has been, "I'm sorry." I had to fight her to walk to school rather than have her drive me, and I never once made my bed until I went away to college. She was perpetual motion, always doing, all for the family. With one exception.

On Fridays, just before sunset, after she had cleaned the house for the sixth and most thorough time that week, taken my brother and me for haircuts, gone to the bakery, and finished cooking, she would actually sit down in the kitchen and paint her nails. I would be drawn in, mesmerized by her attention to herself, while the smells of Sabbath dinner wafted through our home. Then, she would veil her face and light the candles.

Once my brother and I were out of the house, she took a job that she loved, and her life started to expand. But almost as soon as it began to blossom, my brother's wife died suddenly, leaving behind two young children.

Without blinking, Mom took up where she left off, and for the next fifteen years, she raised her grandchildren as her children. Each school day, they would open their lunches and find a loving note inside.

Meanwhile, my dad slowly succumbed to multiple sclerosis and since taking a fall nine months ago, has been mostly confined to a wheelchair.

I usually come to town twice a week to visit and to give them acupuncture treatments. I have learned to not *do* anything, that is, to not wash a dish, dry one, or sweep the floor. As it was during childhood, Mom fights anyone who attempts to help.

Night has fallen, and with it, the phone rings. Mom is calling to tell me about her day.

"This morning, out of the blue, Dad chose to use his walker to go into the bathroom and shave." She sounds mystified and delighted.

And this afternoon my brother took her to the driver's license bureau to apply for a new license.

"I came prepared to have my picture taken," she says, "so I wore a solid sweater instead of a striped one, and I wore a necklace."

But she did not have her picture taken.

"I'm disappointed and I'm also relieved, because I feel that I've become dangerous," she continues. "I just can't see well enough to drive."

I feel a stab in my heart, but without missing a beat, she changes the topic, telling me that she has recently become interested in talk shows addressing self-esteem.

"I'd like for you to tell me about it next time I see you," I say, "but I need to go now."

I hurry to hang up as tears flood my eyes.

Pomp and Circumstances

It is a beautiful picture, cast in amber light, of my son and me in the shower, water flowing off my head and down between our bodies. I am holding him up to the water, all four years of him. My eyes are smiling but weary, my hair has begun to recede, I have a moustache, and I am looking into the camera. His soft eyes are obscured by downturned lids, his complexion is light in contrast to mine, his mouth is sealed, and his head is turned away from mine.

The snapshot reveals the nature of our relationship, already firmly established, that I would spend the next fourteen years desperately trying to change. It is also a picture of a divorce in progress, although the end would still be eight years away.

In the first months after Laibrook was born, I thought we were off to a pretty good start. I would respond to his unhappy times by putting him in his car seat in the '62 Buick Special convertible and taking rides along the Peak-to-Peak Highway with the top down. Coincidentally, Meher Baba disciples Brewer and Shipley would always, it seemed, be singing their Indian anthem to spring, "Witchi-Tai-To," on the radio during those drives. Every time the song came on, he would calm down, so I began to sing it to him in the middle of the night when he would awaken, crying in some unknown pain. I would walk around the cabin with him cradled in my arms.

A few years later, at a winter solstice ceremony, an elderly Pueblo women approached Laibrook from out of nowhere. She laid him down and placed her hands on his abdomen. After several minutes, she proclaimed that she had corrected the position of his liver, which she said had always been tilted and had been a source of great pain.

About the time the shower picture was taken, I started studying with a master Japanese healer. I studied with him by night, and by day, I taught at a prep school. The overload manifested one morning as I lifted Laibrook out of the top bunk. I am fainting, and my last recollection before I collapse into total darkness is throwing him onto the bottom bed.

I didn't recognize it at the time, but now I see that this kind of sacrifice was my inheritance, a 5000-year-old paradigm that I participated in. The agreement was clear: the male would go out into the world for acquisition and posterity; the female would engage in sorcery. And so, I was off on my quest and seeing to my family's needs. In this agreement, some thing--an idea--mirrored by obsessive doing, becomes more important than my loved ones. My children are told, "Your father doesn't mean it" by their mother, but in the end, they hate me for it. Her power lay in the home, a power over her children. And like the biblical Abraham who agrees to exile his "illegitimate" son upon his wife's request, I concede to relinquish the home for the lure of my quest. Abraham also agreed to God's request that he sacrifice his sons. I am enraged at this agreement for her to be the witch and me to be the weary father, head hung low.

Eventually, this pact wore thin for me. I wanted a greater role in parenting and wanted to decrease my work load so that I could be at home more.

But the momentum of our agreement was too great. Laibrook's mother and I separated only months before he turned thirteen.

I silently decided that that year, Laibrook's birthday river trip would serve as my version of his Bar Mitzvah. Ever since I introduced him to river running at an early age, he requested that his birthdays be celebrated with a river expedition. Each successive year became the stage for a more ambitious journey. Previously, we had run the river on single-day trips, but I believed a multi-day trip down a wilderness river would be more suitable for this important "coming-of-age" time. Although most of the outings were fun, this one would turn out to be hell, perhaps in keeping with the entire divorce environment.

I scrambled to surround him with classmates and with adult friends to paddle in two rafts, supporting him as he faced the challenge of a wild river from the solitude of an inflatable kayak. So much for my dreams.

The river sent home the message louder than ever that he did not have any friends. Only occasionally could he coax one of the children to join him in the kayak. Ashore in camp, they played, and he wandered around, alone. His anger and frustration grew by the moment and erupted after an adult confronted Laibrook about trying to control activities in camp. Laibrook physically threatened the man with the burning end of a campfire log. Increasingly, Laibrook's attitude reflected in his performance on the river, and eventually no one wanted to ride in his craft with him.

The last day on the river held the most challenging rapids, but he was engaged in a constant tirade against me, calling me names and telling me how stupid I was. The more I ignored his assaults, the worse things got. His boat went crashing into every obstacle in sight, and we had not even reached the big rapids. An alarm went off inside me. I decided to pull ashore and deflate his boat. When Laibrook saw that I meant business, he quickly sobered up and promised to act respectfully toward the people on the trip and toward the river.

Once his attitude had changed, several of the kids asked if they could ride with him through the big water. I agreed to let one of the boys join him. I observed Laibrook carefully as the boats made final preparations for the big test. At the top of the first rapid, his classmate fell overboard, and Laibrook, in an act of adrenal magnitude, quickly pulled the boy back in the boat and immediately resumed paddling, just in time to avoid some dangerous pour-over holes. He ran the rest of the river flawlessly that day, and as the adults packed up gear at the take-out point, all of the kids played hard. Laibrook was, for that afternoon, one of the gang.

After the divorce, Laibrook dropped his first name in favor of his middle name, Dylan. I moved to another city. Living at the time with his mother, he called one day and asked to live with me. My reaction was mixed. On the one hand, I was sick of the distance that he continually kept from me and of his disdain for my values, beliefs, and ancestry, while praising his mother for hers and saving his warmth and his personal bright side for her. On the other hand, I saw it as an opportunity to break our stalemate. Besides, he was fast approaching his sixteenth birthday, and I was still hot on significant birthdays as rites of passage.

Living together was indeed a mixture of push and pull, breakthroughs and setbacks. In the beginning, he stayed in his room with the door locked or away from the house. I would hear his voice turn animated only when he carried the phone into his room, closed the door, and called his mom. I felt cheated, shortchanged, angry at a triangle that had always been there but that I had conveniently ignored until then. The relationship that was his mother, him, and me had always worked that way.

Gradually, he emerged from his room. He accepted my help in preparing for his driver's license and let me plan a kayak trip down the San Juan river for his birthday. He would do the driving.

On the way to the river, we stopped in the town of Ouray. My nerves were shot from the trip preparation, Dylan's high-speed driving, and ferocious winds, so while he browsed antique stores on the main street, I went for a run along an undulating forest trail through the spectacular San Juan mountains.

When I picked him up, I asked him to join me in the vapor hot spring cave, under the ruins of Ute Chief Ouray's former home. He declined, but I believe that he saw my pain coming to the surface, because he offered to wait while I soaked. It was a selfless act: just ahead lie the "million-dollar highway," a driving challenge he was hoping to meet in daylight.

Fifteen minutes in hot mineral water was all that was required to open the gates. As I came out of the cave and headed toward the shower, the dream I had carried for a family, the ensuing separation, the death of my marriage, my fury at the attitudes that made it all irretrievable, now manifested, in toto, spilling into every nook and cranny of my emotional body. I broke down crying hysterically in the hallway.

Dylan appeared at that instant and asked me what was wrong.

"I don't feel you and your brothers love me," I heard myself say.

He reached out and hugged me. "Of course we love you."

I replied that my physical distance from them had created this feeling.

He stayed nearby and helped me gather my belongings, as I slowly collected myself in the eerily quiet aftermath.

Once back on the road, he handled the van with a new authority as he learned to use the different gears to his advantage, be it climbing or descending. He was even collected enough to take in the scenery, and wheeled us into Durango as the last flecks of twilight dissipated into night.

Over dinner at a brew pub, he added Ouray and Durango to his list of suitable candidates for places to live, while I worked at appearing normal. We agreed that the final two hours of the drive would wait until morning. I have a feeling that I scared him with the shear power of my emotions. He was being friendly, but we did not mention my breakdown. What would I have done if I had ever seen my dad lose it?

For me, our trip down the San Juan was a journey into beauty. For Dylan, it was too windy. On our final evening, I cornered him hiking up Grand Gulch. I asked him why he wasn't ever sad about his mother and I breaking up.

"You never really seemed married," he told me. "Mom did her job, and you did yours. When it ended, I got mad--I don't know why--for a day."

When I asked why he so often gets angry with me, he replied, "I know that I do, but I don't know why."

Two years pass, and we have continued to live together. He has not yet changed his last name to his mother's, although on occasion he's threatened to. He says it's an embarrassment that people automatically know he is Jewish. I have replied without hesitation, but with an inner pain of rejection, that if it would make him happier, he should change his last name.

As we approach the date of his high school graduation, he begins to create his invitation list. He sits down beside me after dinner, and, of course, doesn't ask me to help him. Then, neither did Tom Sawyer ask anyone to help him paint the fence.

As I conjure up names, he responds with complete acceptance, free from his often cynical tendencies. What memories the names bring me: my musician friend who happened to be playing tennis at the hospital courts as we sped up to the entrance that full moon day, then immediately dropped his racquet and ran to join us when our dream of a home delivery manifested in a high-tech Caesarean section; our then-fourteen-year-old neighbor, now a mother of three, who brought her horse for him to ride at his first birthday party; my old climbing, skiing, and kayaking partner whom Dylan would always, from an early age, scold for taking me away from him; teachers he admired; peers who remained his friends over time and distance; his mother's and my families. He has singled out those who have become models for him, and I am impressed.

He is not quite eighteen years old, yet he already carries a deep respect and love for these people. I am humbled. He has lots of friends nowadays. My heart feels full, proud of who he has become, sore with his imminent departure. A lot is being loosed this evening. Fragments begin to stir.

After we finish the list, we work out a schedule for him to do my accounting books in exchange for his car repairs, a speeding ticket, and spending money. We work it out together, unlike our adversarial roles of times past. For me, it is a tribute to the two of us living together, growing together, over these years.

As he heads out to be with friends, he tells me he will be home by ten. He doesn't return until midnight. The breach is a departure for him since he always follows through on our agreements. I immediately call him on it. Although he apologizes once he feels my concern, he has begun to leave; our cord is being cut.

Some tension that existed seemingly forever between us is easing, as each moment calls me to see him anew. I begin to flash back, persistently, to a moment in the hospital on the day after his birth.

Cradling him in my arms, I walked back and forth through the newborn ward, part of me in shock, part of me in wonder, when my trance was broken by the roar of a large black grandmother, who proclaimed, "No doubt about who his father is."

Her words became my koan. No doubt about who I was, but how was I supposed to act? What does a father *do*? That unknown made for a stiff uniform, as the days turned into years, and I looked outward for the answer.

The years brought changes and the opportunity to try on other uniforms, yet only now, as he begins to leave, do I grasp that he and his brothers saw *me* through each and every act, that they were simply waiting for me to be me, no act necessary.

As we converge on graduation day, he pushes the envelope in every conceivable way, and all from a place of hunger, from his natural instinct to individuate. Witness: He stops asking me for permission to wear my clothes, yet I see him in them more than ever. Concurrently, he willingly introduces his friends to me, slowly confides more in me, brings me into his life. Witness: One evening, I delight in playing frisbee with him and his friends, a first.

As the envelope expands, and the rules are ignored or rewritten, I begin to feel a strange sense of freedom. I actually begin to relax. For eighteen years, I would awaken at or before the slightest stirring in the night from his or his brothers' bedrooms. These past two years I would always hear him come home, no matter how late. Yet there are now nights when I do not hear him come in. Telepathic agreements come undone, allowing subterranean feelings to burst to the surface.

A week before the big day, I am engulfed in rage toward his mother--about the way our marriage ended, about broken commitments and broken dreams. The greatest change in me since the divorce is that I no longer judge against my feelings. The rage reveals that I still love her, that I will always love her, and with the revelation, I claim a fragment of myself and feel more able to love him. By the day I am more entranced, simply watching him live his life.

As I move through this passage, my whole sense of time changes. I realize that I do not have forever. Every moment becomes precious. I simultaneously feel older and younger.

But by the time graduation day arrives, I am back on edge, wanting things to go just right, wanting his reception to be good. At the ceremony, I observe that his class is more mature, more worldly than mine was. And that the violence of our civilization now permeates every corner, that they wear blood-stained caps and gowns from classmates' suicides and from brutal beatings, this in a model community.

As they march up to receive their diplomas, I recognize that we live in a world of broken dreams, and with the delusion, comes the pain of reality, and with the suffering, we come in touch with living, finally free to move beyond the limits of a 5,000-year-old agreement and its attendant fantasies.

His reception goes well, but I do not begin to unwind until the guests have gone and his mother and I gravitate to the photo collections and baby albums. These warm me, make me feel grateful for the path that I have walked. We cry together, and in that moment there are no regrets. I walk her out into the evening, hug her, and say, "We did good."

I return alone to the house and find a card for me in the darkened study. It is from an old friend, someone who has always shown up for me. It reads: "Congratulations to you, too, Stu. You've raised yourself a man. What a special thing. Good for you."

And so on this morning after, something has changed for the first time in eighteen years. Once more I am in the newborn ward, and I see the whole picture: I am holding him and I realize that I am where I have always wanted to be, and that there is no need for me to do anything about it, no uniform to wear. I am freely adoring my baby, and on this morning, I do not feel weary. My exile is ending.

As the Crone Flies

May wanes under watery skies. A day for remembering the Crone, for paying her tribute. Webster's calls them old hags. That's only the surface illusion. Underneath lie mystical, undreamed-of currents that run deep.

I met her thirteen months ago, and only now do I begin to understand how to honor my feelings. Too, it was ten years ago this month that I told my teacher I was going out on my own, to make my own mistakes, to find my own truths about healing and about life. Ten years of practice in my work, tradition has it, and then you are a beginner. Cycles.

Where did she come from, and why did I meet her then? The previous winter had been an excruciating one. I had chosen to single parent all of my boys for the school year, and the romantic love relationship of my life was simultaneously ripping apart. By early April I was dragging my body to a treasured vapor cave, seeking closure on the relationship, praying to grasp how to never again fall into the unrequited love trap, and intent upon surrendering to the healing.

I was alone, driving along the interstate toward the cave, when I heard the voice: "You are about to meet one of the most important people in your life." That's all it said. So single-minded was I, so dissociated from my feelings due to my efforts to push away the seemingly endless pain, that my heart did not bother to skip even one beat.

Forty-five minutes later, I was down in the cave, sweat emerging from every pore. Sulfur has historically been associated with the devil. I'd have to agree, because with the breaking sweat came a march of demons, fragments of myself that I had long judged against. Down there in those dark, hot recesses.

Even so, when two women I cannot see sit down in the cave, I immediately realize that one of them is the "important person." I am shy by nature, but I find an opening in their conversation, and soon she and I discover that her best friend is one of my acupuncture patients. I walk into another chamber to cool down under a shower and let out a roar of laughter that I have met her. Some time later, I would find out that upon our meeting, she was feeling giddy, very giddy. But so obsessed am I with my pain, so heartbroken and exhausted, that I walk upstairs and out without saying goodbye. I return to the cave for two more days, then come home feeling a bit more alive.

A week later I feel the curious sensation deep inside of being in love, and by the breath, the feeling grows. It takes me three days to identify the object of my affection, at which time, under the full moon on Good Friday eve, I consider calling her friend, to obtain the Crone's phone number. The phone rings. She tells me that she has been feeling the same way. We agree to meet on the day of the resurrection, at a place along the way to a kayaking trip I've planned with three male friends.

On Easter Sunday morning, I drive through falling snow toward our rendezvous. At the summit of the last mountain pass, a startling event occurs: two spirit helpers who have given me extraordinary support since my divorce (each appearing separately and of their own volition, not at my request) now arrive together for the first time. I knew each of these beings when they were alive, and now they've come to bid me farewell. Their message is simply that I am on my own. In a joyous burst, they are gone forever from my life. I suddenly experience an emptiness that is at once alarming and filled with possibilities. I sob all the way down the pass, mourning the loss of loved ones and feeling wonder at where they may be off to.

I carry these feelings to my destination, to the moment that the Crone and I actually first set eyes on one another. Snow swirls around us at 10,000 feet, and the cold day prompts us to retreat to a motel room, whereupon we do nothing, neither touching nor talking; we simply sit and gaze, spellbound, for hours.

After our time together ends, I push on and arrive at P.'s house that night. Early the next day, the four of us drive relentlessly toward the river. I ask myself if she has come out of a desperation to buffer my pain. "No, she has arrived out of my desire to feel it all, from head to toes." And will we hold hands when we jump off the cliff? What I know for certain is that I am not in control of this one.

The first two days on the river, I feel ravaged, laid bare, awkward in a tight, stiff body, unusually slow to adapt, to shrug off the neuroses of day-to-day city existence. Indecision reigns at every bend in the river, a dangerous reflection in white water. I paddle to survive and when in camp, feel unable to cope. I realize that I am preoccupied with the Crone. The beautiful wilderness where I carry out the drama simply exists, indifferent to my angst.

On the second night, I cook a good dinner, which we eat in the dark. Just before lying down, I am moved to reposition my sleeping bag so that my head aligns with the north star, and soon I fall gently asleep to the sound of a columbine-tiered waterfall.

In the morning, I awaken to the howl of coyotes and recall that the Crone has made three requests of me: to be impeccable, to be one-hundred percent present whenever I am with her, and to leave the toilet seat down.

As I muse, B., softly smiling his ever-present smile, surprises me by delivering a cup of tea to my outdoor bed. Feeling well rested, I see that we are camped in a Zen garden, that perfection surrounds me.

Still, I am aware of a separation between me and these three men. They work together as teachers at a private school and stand aligned in their cosmology. They are sensitive men, yet restrained in their emotions. But, who am I to talk?

My first paddle strokes on the water this day reveal that I am merging with the river--now I am remembering why I journey here. Fear yields to my passion for experiencing the texture of the ride, for inhaling my surroundings, for listening to the mood of the river, for having fun. Now I am paying attention, coming unglued, taking some risks.

I descend over a steep drop and suddenly find the stern of my kayak perpendicular to the water, the bow pointing straight up at the sky. I am going end over end backwards. Without thinking or wincing, my roll is there, fluid, and I am delirious with the moment, upright again, howling, and gliding downstream.

More rapids, more ecstasy, and then we agree to stop for lunch. I sit on a sand beach eating, baking in the southwest sun, and savoring my life in this wondrous place. Lunch conversation is filled with the playful energy of the river, as we men tease one another in a consciously jocular way.

In the light of this spring afternoon, the river surface transforms into a dark satin sky bursting with twinkling sun drops. Floating freely, I witness the wonder as a child.

Toward day's end, K. finds a good wave for playing in and beckons me to try it. I observe that the wave has entrapment potential, but I join him anyway. Soon I am upside down and disoriented. After three attempts and on my last bit of air, I roll back up. I back off a bit, feeling ready for the campsite we had agreed upon at lunch time.

When we arrive, I am quick out of my boat, surveying the site, feeling happy to be here, but sensing a queer resistance behind me. My companions are still in their boats. B. explains that if we camp here, then tomorrow will make for a long day on the river, and that there is still plenty of daylight to paddle another three miles to the next canyon.

I feel surprised, and I feel their agreement field. My body wants to stop. My heart is set on this site. Then, from inside me comes the voice of reason: "You need to learn to compromise, to work better with a group."

When I return to my boat I am immediately tentative with the river. I am separate from my feelings, back in my mind, and so I avoid the big water.

At our new camp, called Yankee Canyon, I lay my sleeping bag under an outcropping. An owl begins to hoot into the night. At breakfast, P. speaks passionately about the crunch on the teachers in his system, and of how these teachers are people who inflate their self-importance for the cause, and how it ultimately kills them. Meanwhile, I reflect that today my ex-wife turns forty, and remember, as I do too often, how suddenly the end came.

The day presents ever larger rapids, and we descend without incident. Then, at the last rapid of consequence, at the last possible moment, it happens: I punch through the great diagonal reflex wave, and all that remains is for me to brace, to use my paddle to support myself at the eddyline. In this instant, doubt rules.

I do not brace, and so over I plunge into a dark web. The tempo immediately shifts from the crashing din above to an eerie slow-motion world filled with ominous surroundings. Panicked, I try to roll too quickly, bringing my head up first instead of last, and back down

I go. As I set up for my second attempt, I hear my
helmet crack on a rock. Next, I feel a sharp blow on my
left shoulder; now, my life is on the line.

I channel all of my attention into the roll. I am aware
of tentacles all around me, still very much in slow
motion. Pain screams through my body as I roll upright,
back into the froth and frenzy. I paddle for my life to the
shore, where I am greeted with grave concern, healing
touch, and homeopathic remedies.

K. tells me that had I not rolled, I would likely have
been trapped between two boulders. I reflect on how I
have rolled so many times yet never before been injured
kayaking, and on how I have never before encountered
that kind of darkness.

In my state of shock, I turn philosophical, on how
the shoulder carries the burden, the sacrifice, perhaps for
the payoff of posterity, perhaps not. And how, at that
crucial juncture, my mind and my body were in
opposition. I am drawn back to the previous afternoon,
when I overrode my instinct and feelings and chose to
march on, ever the good soldier.

But no amount of thinking can keep me from the
agony of endlessly more paddling, and at its peak, I cry,
"No more." I rage, "No more," over and over again. I
contract as even riffles on the water threaten to devour
me.

We camp on an island of exquisitely smooth boulders. B. and P. tell me of the giant meteor they witnessed the night before at Yankee Canyon. K. remarks that we agreed to a men's trip so that we could fart together sooner. Each of them takes a turn at giving my shoulder care. Soon I am sleeping.

In the dreamtime, I find myself in a five-story school building, round and open in the center. In sweeping gestures, I throw the library display books on the floor as the students cheer me on.

I awaken with a clear response to the dream. I associate the school with my companions. The books represent ideas, far removed from the truth of each moment, a truth which requires that our minds be in partnership with our bodies and with our feelings. The four-fold universe just won't cut it. We need to address life from the void, the fifth dimension. Hence, the five-story building.

On our last day on the river, I paddle with the heaviness of having come so close to breaking through the violence of separation, of having been in this place before, and of having failed at the crux moment to show up for myself. Despair.

Then, around a bend, perched on a dead tree branch overhanging the river, and not ten feet above me, sits a bald eagle, waiting for me, for us. Spellbound, I am the first to pass. Its gaze is fixed on me.

From deep inside, I hear: "There will be moments in the future when you will fail to support yourself, but your feelings will rise up stronger each time, until you move in constant harmony, free from further danger of self-harm and self-destruction. You have passed through the door to the living. The light will only continue to grow from here. You will become softer and stronger each day, and happiness will fill your life."

I ask: "What about the Crone?"

"Two gather. Pay attention. Stay with your feelings on this one. Honor them."

A female rain (without thunder and lightning) is falling freely now, thirteen months later, and my time with the Crone has ended. She unflinchingly held the light for me as she showed me how to come to my feelings, and then taught me how to honor them. My gratitude to her, to this extraordinary soul, is endless. A month ago, my feelings told me that the time had come for me to leave the relationship, to practice standing upright, to honor my inner teacher, to make my mistakes, and to find my truth in each moment. On my own. Cycles.

Part Two

Hairapy

The salon is humming on a warm, brilliant Saturday afternoon at the peak of autumn. I willingly forego the enticing weather and walk inside. Kristina instantly appears, looking blond, tan, and ever-ravishing. She greets me with a hug that tells me I have been missed.

Today, I do not stop to put on one of the salon T-shirts, even though we have a standing joke about the time she soaked my shirt while washing my hair. I settle back, and she begins to shampoo my hair and massage my scalp.

"You always look great and healthy, Stuart," she tells me, as I relax into her touch.

In our usual laser-like way we feel out how we are each faring with our deepest concerns. Little wonder that the eyes around us slowly but surely turn our way. We've grown used to it over these four years.

As I stand up and transfer to another chair, I reflect on how far I have travelled from the days when I would suffer through haircuts at the hands of somber men carrying hidden rage that seeped out through their hands, men with overstuffed bellies pushing uncomfortably against my elbows. And how virtually all talk in the room, low-pitched, somber, and sporadic though it was, was directed to hunting and fishing. I was fidgety, too nervous to sit still, not for a moment trusting these men with the sharp tools, and so I often served as the boobie prize for some rookie barber. I would barely breathe in order to numb my feelings in those dark places. In some other lifetime.

Today, as always, Kristina meets me in ritual. Our encounter is deeply intimate as we look at one another mostly via the mirror, instead of directly. From this indirect exchange emerge heightened feelings, where every word carries a sensual, yet sober, multi-dimensional flavor, becomes fuel for the dance. There is a movement to it, or, rather, movements--circles to the left, circles to the right, circles joining. Satisfying, balanced, not about teasing or flirting.

I met Kristina shortly after I moved here. Until then, my ex-wife had always cut my hair--curly, black hair that I hated all my life. After all, I was ineligible to become a surfer or a Beatle. And, it was a dead give-away for my Jewishness. I tried every conceivable way to straighten it. Then, only days before my marriage would explode, I decided to let what remained have its way, to be my mane.

When I moved to this Colorado town, I arrived intent upon releasing my carefully-cultivated persona. I came here to create a new life, together with a woman I was deeply in romantic love with. No, she never offered to cut my hair, and I never asked her to, for out of my subconscious came the name "Delilah," over and over, once we began living together. Actually it was she who discovered Kristina, the mystic from Germany.

So, I took a deep breath and walked into a catchy-name hair-styling salon, peopled mostly by women. From the start, it felt good; I found manna.

Kristina and I have convened fairly regularly since, and discuss things mostly spiritual, always meaningful. She is extremely gifted in cutting my hair, and her ethnic ancestry has served to heal my biases against the German people.

"Funny that you should come in today, because only an hour ago I decided that today would be my final day cutting hair," Kristina tells me. She will be moving on to her own business on a South Sea island. I do not say so, but I, too, feel my time here coming to a close.

We dive deeper into our meeting. She talks of her new business and life on the island as a vision, and of her commitment to that vision.

"To have a vision can often be pain-causing," she remarks, "because you must then be willing to meet all challenges that arise."

Lately, she has been watching movies about visionary individuals and groups, about their trials and tribulations. I am with her, word for word, and I add that without a vision, our lives are carried out in the numbing arena of delusion, rather than reality.

"Yes," she adds, "and if we go without [a] vision, then we invest energy in a love partner instead, and it is only a matter of time until it sours."

Here, our eyes respond by meeting in the mirror, and they reflect the pain of that truth.

Of late, she has also been watching violent movies which she had avoided for so long, because she had refused to acknowledge that she was "cut from the same violent strand as the characters in those movies." She confesses this to me in close, as she trims around my ears and goes for the final touches, the artist possessed. Her words become soft utterances in my ears, virtual whispers, these confessions of her humanness. I am flooded with her vulnerability, touched by her willingness to see.

And now she begins to stall, to draw our meeting out, as she cuts hair by single hair, savoring our connection with all her deliberate mastery. She talks about assisting in a healing therapy program from which she graduated but has never actively practiced.

"God, how depleted my classmates [who have been practicing] are now," she says. "I've spent the last two years being filled instead of giving it all away."

Again, Kristina's words hit the mark, as I am feeling more depleted than ever from my acupuncture practice.

She brings out a small mirror for me to examine her work. She enjoys my desire to see what she has done, since most men, she says, don't want to take the time to look.

I notice that the hint of a bald spot four years ago has come into full manifestation. I also see that it has not in the least dimmed the juice between us.

Kristina turns the talk to spirituality, to a teacher she has recently discovered. I listen, but we are not aligned on this one. I feel her wanting my approval, but say nothing.

I arise and for the first time feel awkward. I will not see her here next time; our future is uncertain. Over these years, we have occasionally entertained moving our relationship into another realm, but then my seer would instruct me to keep it here, because this is where our greatest appropriateness lies. This has been one situation where I have actually honored my intuitive knowing, and I have prospered.

She tells me that she will call me when she returns from Bali. I reflect that between our last visit and this one, I have met a woman with whom I feel freer, happier, more fully myself each day. Standing here, looking directly at Kristina, I realize that a time has ended and that another has begun. My awkwardness transforms into gratitude as we hug goodbye, and Indian summer beckons me back outside.

Running with Ghosts

I am running, today along the edge of the Pacific Ocean near a place made famous by swallows. Mary and I set out a week ago to attend a wedding in San Diego, travelling by car so that we could explore the West for a new home. We were in search of a place untainted, a bright spot apart from the disintegration. We had ideas about parts of Utah and Arizona, and quickly realized, as we witnessed hate spewing out on remote small town street corners, that skinheads and survivalists have been seeking out these places, too.

The truth surrounds us: there is nowhere to go; anywhere, that is, to find comfort from the storm, in the waning days of this civilization. At every turn, we have been confronted by the harsh reality of breakdown, of a creation gone out of control, of existence played out from a place of extreme separation. Numb, heartless, violent.

I have joined right in by looking for the things that I do not like about Mary, then pushing her away. When I allow myself to feel her, our baby who grows inside of her, my children, special friends, and myself, I see overlapping spheres of energy that join to form something much greater and more formidable than the singular me. But I immediately back off, fearing the loss of my identity. I back off even though it feels good, like my true home, an organism that is at once totally familiar to some part of me, yet completely foreign to my phenomenal memory.

I am running in search of quiet, to ground from too much driving. The sky and ocean create a world of sparkling white and powder blue. I flirt with the breaking surf as I run, while the ocean and the sun comfort me, soothe my nerves.

As I begin to clarify, I ask, "What is it that I cling to?" Not far ahead lies the answer. I always run without my contact lenses, which turns people into unspecific blurs, and today along this very stretch of ocean, I see her, or rather, her ghost. With the sighting, I plead with God for just one more chance to return to my life with this woman.

Oh, my deepest romantic vision, which I still seek outside of myself, a dedication to drama, a desire to change the unchangeable, to heal the unhealable. Willful beyond belief, this part of me does not seek harmony, it seeks to conquer, and in that blind, insatiable drivenness, disregards even its own well-being. In this mode, I accept that she will in turn constantly batter me. But, I ask, "What am I to do? I crave her style." It is a feeling, a motive vibration that is ancient, an inheritance of this lifetime. It is a desire that, at those times when I have succumbed, has caused me to override all other feelings, all inclination to well-being, and chase the wailing siren, gawk at the firecracker fuse lit in my hand.

Time and distance fly today. I have run perhaps three miles and now begin to feel in flow, as each step becomes more effortless. I arrive at the first break in the row of beach houses, a space of perhaps a hundred yards, enough room to sit and breathe. Even the powerful trains that frequent this stretch do not deter me from enjoying the day, and as I begin to return to myself, I find that I am in limbo: part of me is attached to the pain of my unrequited past; part of me is clearly on a new course and dedicated to a life beyond the game.

At summer solstice, Mary and I separately and simultaneously chose to stop participating in romances, the draining world of constant opposition. We each decided we'd rather be alone than engage in another relationship of that kind. When we joined, we did so without fantasy. But inherited attitudes have their own momentum, and mine now entertains the ghosts of a dying civilization.

A passing train pulls me out of my meditation, but only a little, thanks to the power of the elements at this splendid spot. Now I remember: In quitting "fatal attractions," Mary and I made room for a force that recognized our desire to go beyond the conventional paradigm.

It was the same force that brought about an unplanned pregnancy early in our relationship. While part of me was angry with God for playing tricks on us, I was also watching Mary step into her full womanhood. And I was experiencing an astonishing transformation myself. Unlike pregnancies earlier in my life, when I was still seeking my identity, this time, I felt lighter and more alive, more relaxed, instead of tight with increased survival responsibility. Old wounds--my history with fathering and family--have risen for the healing. Frustrations and shattered dreams have surfaced as grief and rage. Over these years, I had given up on being a family. I was going to be a parent, a father specifically, and through that, do the best I could, albeit in the sacrificial mode. Now, with reality as my guide, I am no longer a victim of my past. Now, everything is possible.

With the onset of the pregnancy, our priorities and sense of direction began shifting beyond the known and out of our control. Instead of being pulled around by the phenomenal, we increasingly looked in, not out, for our understanding of how to live, until we came to just one certainty: each day more veils of delusion would be shredded.

By staying in touch with reality, we began to return to ourselves. We discovered a world of increasing fulfillment from one moment to the next.

But as the changes grew more intense, we backed off and contracted into our heads; we separated from our gift and looked outward for the answers. We got in the car and headed west.

The wedding was the last straw for me--a death ritual, a mirror of the heartlessness we had driven back into. We all silently agreed to make the groom's mother the villain for this ritual. Her every action and attitude took center stage; she became the object for blame, for our collective unhappiness. No one said or did anything to change the script. In containing the hate, we also shut out spontaneity and all other feelings, turning the wedding into a mechanical playing out of carefully orchestrated actions. I watched Mary's face transform from the blooming radiance of early pregnancy into tightly drawn severity. What greater form of barbarism do we practice than the collective lie?

Mary and I became more polarized by the day until after the wedding, when she cried for an end to the madness, knowing only that she wanted to be at the ocean.

I relax into the warm open air and soft sand. I realize I'm accepting my past. The ghosts may come and go, but they will not pull me away from my new life, from my choice to be full and free.

I feel calmer, happier, ready to turn around. I breathe more easily and I notice that my shadow is looking more upright than when the run began.

The beautiful beach houses, one by one, project a sense of emptiness, as if they are uninhabited, a stark contrast to how I am now feeling. Where is everyone, I wonder?

In no time, Mary greets me, and as usual she shows up, heart open to our journey. I am back. She tells me that my running form looked nice and relaxed. As we hug, I am called to her belly; I feel blessed.

* * * * *

For the next few days, we stay at a nearby, virtually empty, terrifically nourishing, hot spring resort, and continue to return to ourselves. Brake trouble on the car conspires to keep us at the spa until parts arrive, until we are rested and back on course.

A few days later, at home, the morning news reports that devastating fires are raging all around the area we

have just been, that a sniper has killed three in San
Diego, and that youth gang killings are skyrocketing in
Southern California suburban counties.

Autumn Air

Just like old times, Dad, Mom, and I are going for a ride in the mountains. The folks have not been out to see the changing colors this year, and as the leaves begin to fall, a hovering blast of winter threatens to bring them all to the ground.

As usual these days, I am at the wheel, while Dad sits shotgun, and Mom positions herself behind my seat. The old Buick reflects Dad's condition, a far cry from when his cars ran in states of perfect maintenance, the pride of his life. Now, the heater and defroster are crippled by a broken core element and leaky hoses. They could spew poisonous fumes into the passenger compartment, so I leave them off.

The low cloud cover lends an iridescent beauty to the deciduous trees, and as yet I see no precipitation. So far, so good. Mom is exuberant at each new stand of trees, while Dad remains silent, eyes fixed straight ahead.

"Look at them, honey!" she exclaims.

"I've never cared for fall," he replies, "because that's when everything dies."

In times past I would have interjected with a meta-physical remark about transformation and metamorpho-sis, as opposed to death, but today I keep on driving, higher into the mountains.

I fumble with the A.M.-only radio dial, and land a sports talk show. The country is still in shock in the wake of Michael Jordan's retirement yesterday; people can only ask "why?". "I just feel that I don't have anything to prove," he said. "The desire just isn't there." His words echo my own. Of late, when I come home from my acupuncture practice, I keep telling Mary that it was boring, something I never before affixed to that work. My capacity to diagnose and to treat has continued to expand, my ego has grown healthier with the work, yet I have become desperately bored. In great part, the satisfaction that I derived from the people I treat has faded. I realize that I am perceived differently than I had previously thought, that their interest in me is purely from their own need. Somehow, my humanness is not recognized. At the same time, I have moved toward a more detached stance, simultaneously more removed and more present in treatments.

Dad brings me back to the ride as he instinctively reaches to adjust the temperature controls.

"We need to leave them off, Dad, because the hoses haven't been fixed yet."

A year and a half ago, on May 1, he took a fall and hit his head. Two days later, he was incontinent, could no longer walk, and his short-term memory was gone, this sensual, humble man of over-sensitive temperament. In an instant, his slow descent over an adult lifetime into multiple sclerosis turned sudden. On May Day, the Beltane, a day for planting, for elves and fairies, for the union of male and female. Since then, Mom has taken complete care of him.

She is loving the ride, and the car has not been driven on a highway in a long time, so I choose to open it up, to drive higher, to push the envelope of the looming storm.

Soon condensation forms on the front window, and Dad again reaches for the controls. I ask Mom for some Kleenex.

"Here, Sol, give this to Stu," she says.

"Give it to him yourself," he replies.

I find myself laughing hard at his words, because I realize that Mom and Dad are taking their relationship to the limit, playing it out to its end.

"He's been acting this way the last few days," she tells me.

Funny, but whenever we are together, he is present, not in the polite and patronizing sense of the word, but in a really deep way, more than ever. I believe that he got bored a long time ago, when he backed off from risk, at a time when his creative juices were making inventions faster than he could patent them. No self-esteem, therefore how could his inspirations have any value? At that juncture, he opted for a life of indentured servitude, working for my grandfather, Mom's father, fitting rental tuxedos. And he fueled it with thirty, no kidding, cups of coffee a day.

"How's work, Mr. Stu?" (his pet name for me). This is a question he asks routinely. The answer he looks for is how busy I am, am I still making a living? I tell him that I am busy, too busy.

"Well, you can be grateful for that," he responds perfunctorily.

It is when we turn the subject to my writing that he always perks up, turns animated and attentive, remembers all of my work. I tell him that I have not been writing lately and that I miss it.

"Good, I can't wait to hear what you come up with," he replies.

I sense pure appreciation, and immediately feel compelled to write.

Just ahead, in the mist, I recognize a familiar mountain park, a place from another time, from my childhood, from a time peopled with Mom's family, now long gone. I stop the car and call Mom out into the invigorating mountain afternoon. In contrast to the air, the ground feels tired, overused. Camera in hand, I ask her to strike a batting pose at a spot that once served as home plate for our extended family picnics. Meanwhile, Dad remains in the car.

Mom and I share memories about what went on here, then return to the car. Dad immediately turns distant, dissociates from the subject. He first came west with his brother-in-law-to-be, because he knew how to fix flat tires, and Jack didn't. On that trip, he fixed twenty flat tires, met his beloved, and unhesitatingly waved goodbye to Cleveland and to the farm.

And good riddance, since it was at the family farm that he one day broke a glass jug containing gasoline while refilling the farm's power supply. In short order, the garage/electrical plant, the barn, and the dance hall were consumed by the conflagration. Not long after that, he was standing with a girlfriend on the second story back porch of his mother's house in Cleveland when the railing gave way and he crashed to the ground, to a skull fracture. It was the same house where his father died, when Dad was five years old.

As we drive away from the mountain park, I recognize his pain, his disillusionment with the life that he has lived. I unhesitatingly attempt to ease his pain, as always, by changing the subject to his greatest passion: women. When it's just the two of us, we often talk about matters of deep intimacy, something that he is keen on. But today, short-term memory gone, he asks me if I have a new girlfriend. I sigh at my habitual rescue efforts.

We stop for a late, warming lunch in a cozy mountain town restaurant, then drive home against the now-steady snowfall. The sports talk show comes back into range, and I reflect on how Michael Jordan used competition to explore the ways of energy, how at his best, he appeared to defy gravity, to soar above all others. As for the public, while it was deeply appreciative and made him a hero without peer, it was also fickle and insatiable; it always wanted more. He recognized that at the core the adulation was empty: he was perceived as an object, not a human being.

My guess is that his father's death was the final straw, that perhaps the one man who unconditionally loved to see Michael Jordan fly was gone. Deep inside, the balance shifted.

So absorbed am I, that only the stink of poisonous fumes brings me back. In my absence, Dad got to the temperature controls, and now I feel nauseated. My internal pump, primed for toxin release after fourteen years of acupuncture practice, starts churning the poisons inside me, and I struggle to focus on the slick road.

We arrive at their home, at my childhood home, before dark, before rush hour. As I push the wheelchair inside, Dad breaks into the grin that he has always had for me, that conveys his deep affection for me, that says what he is afraid to say.

"It's been a great afternoon," he tells me.

Soon, I'm off, intent on releasing the poisons and on returning to my writing, thankful for who my folks are.

A Grand Idea

Sunday, November 7. I awaken restlessly to an ancient frustration in my body. I have decided to meet Aaron, my oldest son, in Japan next month. Before he left for his studies in Nepal, we considered the possibility of rendevouzing on the Asian island country at semester's end.

It was a good idea in that it would bring us together in a place new to both of us, which would help keep us present and minimize our outdated pictures of who we are. It would also serve to ease him back to "normalcy." It was a good *idea*. Mary encouraged me to go, just when I was feeling ambivalent about it due to cost and some not-yet-conscious considerations. So I proceeded to make airplane reservations and began planning the hot springs, hiking trails, and sacred places that he and I could explore.

A few days later, I called Aaron and told him I was coming. I immediately sensed his uneasiness. He told me that Thai Airways no longer offered the free option of laying over in Japan. In addition, the return date from his trek to the Everest base camp was mired in third-world uncertainty, making our meeting date iffy. But when I had committed to going, I opened a door, and for the first time in a very long while my juices stirred in anticipation of a country and a culture with which I felt a deep connection. Of course we could make it happen; anything was possible.

That my juices were stirring about *anything* marked a big shift. Since Mary became pregnant a few months ago, each day I have felt less pull from anything outside myself, less attraction to any kind of doing, less than I have in my life.

After Aaron heard the excitement in my voice, and after I offered to pay for the extra plane fare, he declared that he would make it all work and would fax me soon with the details.

My growing non-attachment had made life quiet, a strange, uneasy sort of quiet that comes when there is nothing left to fill that place inside that has always looked outward for gratification. The phone, a constant connection for me to the messiah's possible return, always busy, grew virtually silent. Restaurants felt hard and empty of real nourishment. Most people around me, friends included, began to appear self-obsessed. Movies and books spoke the language of violence, desperation, and unrequited existence. Mary was having the same experience.

When any given moment wasn't enough for me, I searched the gamut of my imagination for a fix. Nothing provided one: not new wilderness challenges, not new angles on my work, not sexual fantasies, not even a new nirvana place to which I could plan a move home.

Japan, then, became a window, a desire reawakened, a part of myself waiting to be discovered, out there. I was already beginning to smell the countryside, to walk in the realm of Mount Fuji, to savor the art and architecture over elegant tea, to come undone in mountain outdoor hot springs, to drift into Oriental ryokan-inspired dreamstates. Now I was cooking. Once again, I had something to *look forward* to.

Meanwhile, Mary was gobbling up books on pregnancy and contacting prospective midwives. I told myself that I could do it all, that I could be all things to everyone, could make them all happy and still get my way. Yet, virtually by the breath, the more I researched the trip, the more I felt myself pushing, living life beyond balanced boundaries. With the decision to make the journey came a sudden time crunch. Looking forward was wrenching me out of the now. Gone was the strange quiet, replaced by a noisy, nervous mind.

Strangest of all, as I looked ahead, I began to realize that I was seeing *me* in all of those exotic places, not Aaron and me. The unique, titillating phenomena had me by the balls. So the old, familiar frustration mounted, until this morning when it reached the breaking point.

In the shower, I yell and scream, expressing the frustration that has been building, releasing it from my nervous system.

At breakfast, I tell Mary that I believe we have been in collusion (co-illusion?) on this one. We are committed to building a home, a family, I say, and going to meet Aaron would pull me away from her at a vital time in our pregnancy and in our family building. We had gone on override to facilitate my trip.

"What I have been experiencing is what happens when I leave my center," I tell Mary. "I want some good alone time to focus on Aaron and me, and this trip is not about that. I'm not going."

At 10 P.M. I place a call half-way around the world. Aaron sounds edgy, in contrast to the great happiness he has been experiencing during his time in Nepal.

"Hi, Stu. I just spent the morning blowing up at a couple of travel agents, but after classes I plan to go down and confront them."

In an instant, the truth flies in: "We're pushing the river on this one, Aaron."

His relief is immediate, and I feel the tension lift as if we are in the same room.

"You know, Stu, all I really want is some alone time with you as soon as I get back."

I tell him that indeed we will have it, that I love him and miss him, and that he can get back to being where he is.

Our conversation over, I happily return to the strange quiet.

In Search of the Tenth Mountain

*Two men, deep in the Colorado back-
country, skiing in the shadow of the legendary Tenth Mountain Division. A
journey at its climactic, crux passage
across a ridge above treeline during a
whiteout. A two-mile land/skyscape on a
colorless day: another world, a good
place for a life-death drama, an easy
realm to get lost in, ending at a virtually
invisible cornice, twenty to thirty feet
vertical. Lose our bearings or one step
too far, and . . .*

We are nearing the jump-off point for a dream
journey of mine. H.C., a superb backcountry skier, will
balance out my oldest, but still-green, sons on a right of

passage: Aaron, fresh back from a semester in Nepal, loaded with trepidation about reentering our culture and losing his newfound sense of purpose and quietude, and Dylan, moving away from home for the first time. The two of them are getting an apartment together. And I am about to become a father for the fifth time. The four of us are planning to ski a part of the Tenth Mountain Hut and Trail System.

I made the hut reservations several months earlier after both boys agreed to the journey based upon my inspiration. Now, the stage is beautifully set, dramatically cast. I imagine the three of us getting closer, more intimate, and feeling more alive from supporting one another on a journey that promises to take them to their known capacity and beyond. I relish in anticipation our final night--a full moon, at a hut with a sauna. And I have my first choice for supporting me: H.C., who exudes confidence in the wilderness, to a fault.

My first clue that something is "off" comes shortly after Dylan takes his first permanent-appearing job and is put in charge of inventory for the very week of the trip. A circumstantial, passive-aggressive bow-out, I angrily observe. Then, comes the meeting that I call with the remaining two participants to discuss trip logistics. I tape it, anticipating a high-charged, giddy good time. I neglect, however, to serve coffee on that Sunday morning, and upon replaying the tape, it sounds as if no one but me showed up. Perhaps I should have scheduled an evening gathering and offered beer.

I begin to regret having planned the trip. Dylan reminds me that I often felt this way when I became over-responsible in preparing for wilderness journeys.

At the meeting, H.C. appears preoccupied--over-burdened by work and by concern for his ailing mother. Aaron gives the adventure lip service, but his actions later in the week are clearly dissociated from any clear commitment: Our agreement to practice backcountry skiing technique and for him to help procure trip food falls into a black hole.

Another warning bell sounds two days before our scheduled departure when we go to the store to reserve Aaron's skis. He opts against learning how to put on his climbing skins, saying he will do it when he picks up the skis. As we drive home, I feel drained of energy and realize that I have been doing his preparation for him. I keep quiet, hoping for a change in attitude, but time and momentum are clearly against this as he drifts off more with each breath, empty of passion.

He spends the ensuing time socializing, and on the night before the trip, calls me from a friend's house in another town to say that he is on his way home to pack.

"It's too late, Aaron. Your actions have spoken for you. This trip would have tested you to your limits had you been properly prepared."

I hear silence and feel the shock of his sudden sobriety on the other end. He sobbingly agrees, saying that he is coming home to help me however he can. Once off the phone, I vow to stop initiating wilderness experiences for the guys. If they ask me, that's another matter.

When Aaron returns, he tells me that he had been feeling fear and a sense of danger around the journey. He also says that his friends' response to my decision was that I was full of shit and that the privilege of youth is irresponsibility. Aaron says he disagreed.

I urge him to use the days ahead for solitude instead of hurrying to be with friends.

"Be alone," I tell him. "Rest and contemplate your return to this country. Set your intentions."

He promises that he will, and we embrace, each more vulnerable for the experience. He presents some of his treasured survival gear for me to use. I thank him and promise that I will tell him goodbye in the morning.

I awaken early Monday feeling ready, for what I cannot say, in spite of a nagging chest condition threatening to go bronchial. For me, the best cure for any ailment has always been wilderness. Give me cold, rain, snow, wind, hail, blistering sun. Only one condition: let it be in wilderness, and I'll get well every time. This is not a macho declaration; it is a revelation about my nervous system's deepest needs.

The van is loaded, but first, important business beckons. I awaken Dylan to hug him goodbye, the last time prior to his leaving home. Instinctively, he reaches up, arms open wide, and pulls me down, part my baby, part a man, with more feeling than I can recall. Gifted with surprise, I experience deep delight.

"Be careful, Dad," he says, "and have a great time."

On I go to Aaron's bedroom and find myself running my fingers through his curly hair. He is resting deeply, clearly happy to be home in bed. He, too, tells me to be careful and that he loves me, before sinking back into deep sleep.

The morning air carries a balmy quality for late January. H.C. appears relieved to hear that Aaron is not coming. His underspoken and deeply intuitive response tells me that we are being well guided, that the Tenth Mountain trails now beckon only the two of us, and that it's just right.

But we are far from being in synch. H.C. offers to follow Mary and me for the drive, but two hundred yards down the road, I decide to change the agreement. I reason that because I like to drive faster than he does, H.C. would feel more comfortable setting the pace. Although he did not, in his great Swedish reserve, say

so, my assumption was wrong. Along the way, we stop
for an unannounced pregnancy pee stop, whereupon
H.C., losing sight of us in his mirror, pulls over. As we
pass him by, he is picking something up off the floor,
and I end up running a quarter mile back up the interstate
to reconnect. He jokes that we are on an ill-fated
journey, to which I do not reply. His words strike an
old, shadowy chord.

We drop H.C.'s truck at our journey's projected end
point, and he joins us for the ride to the starting point.
The week-long weather forecast promises a heavy snow
dump in the high country, maybe two. He comments
that a group of his friends recently made the same tour
we have planned, and that a huge snowfall made it
impossible for them to reach their hut destination one
night, mandating a bivouac in bitter cold weather. Why,
I wonder, does he always laugh when he relates such
stories?

As we draw closer to being out there, my trepidation
grows. Life in warm cars and houses looks increasingly
appealing, and on the other hand, some greater part of
me is ready to glide out into a mystery, scripted by a
force much greater than me. That is what brought me
here. It's what makes this trip different. I am more
aware of the opposition within me than in the past, when
fear would fill me until I would either push it away and
let my overriding will whip me onward, or I would back

out at the last minute. Today, I savor the challenge and I acknowledge the fear. I have room for both.

I would also normally be flooded with guilt about why a father of four persists in risk-taking journeys, or I would lash myself a few good ones for going out to have fun while the world remains an imperfect place. Today, I am free to simply enjoy the experience.

I do not like to be apart from Mary, but I feel that now I must. She reads to me from a book we have been sharing aloud, while H.C. gazes out the window. But I am preoccupied with the persistent images of a day twenty years ago, one that H.C. and I would not be denied. In those days, we lived from journey to journey. The West was a younger, cleaner, and seemingly simpler world. We were outlaws, drawn there to become whole, although we weren't conscious that we were broken (we thought that was everyone else). We had just created a continuing education program for the university--half scamming to live our days on rivers, in mountains, and in deserts; half committed to bringing our wounded generation to nature for the healing.

On that day, we decided on a ski tour over the Continental Divide as a nice way to flow from an early-morning business meeting into our passion. We encountered unusually warm sun on the abundant new snow, and when we arrived at a potential avalanche field, we were only marginally cautious. H.C. went first. We agreed that I would give him a leeway of a hundred yards. Halfway into it, the slope came screaming down at him, and he had time only to turn his skis downhill and attempt a race. His cool astonished me, but the snow was winning. At the last moment, he skied into a tree and wrapped his arms around it, buried up to his shoulders, but quite alive.

After spending considerable time and energy digging him out, we debated about whether or not to continue. The threat of avalanche was mostly behind us, more climbing to the top of the Divide and the descent down the old trail still ahead. The sun was moving past its overhead position. We did not for a moment seriously consider retreat. "Onward," we cried.

By the time we reached the eastern slope of the Great Divide, the world before us lay in shadows. The "trail" had long since gone the way of no use and what remained now was covered by ice and was precipitous at best. But it was the best alternative around, so H.C. instructed me to kick my boots into each step in order to create a hold for footing, since we had not even considered bringing crampons. Somewhere on the descent, my weariness revealed itself. I neglected to kick in, and suddenly I was spinning down the ice face, heading for a long drop over a ledge onto a frozen alpine lake. I did indeed see my whole life before me and knew that I was going to die, when, from nowhere, I managed a self-arrest by stabbing my ski poles into the frozen surface.

This time, we broke into long hysterical laughter, the two of us having waved death off separately on the same day. By the time we were ready for the last four miles, shadow had given way to dusk, and was quickly turning to night. The trail was rated expert, and we skied most of it in total darkness, but it felt easy compared to the rest of the day. We met my wife at trail's end. She had almost left to call Mountain Rescue, but she knew us, she knew our style, and she knew deep down that we were all right.

My reminiscing is interrupted by H.C.'s report from the back seat: "According to the map, we begin just over this bridge."

I turn the van onto a trailhead parking lot, at the remains of the Tenth Mountain Division training center, Camp Hale. We step out into the mountains.

With my gear virtually ready, there is little room for my customary dawdling. I sense H.C.'s surprise at my readiness, since he more than anyone has stood by me through this neurosis of mine over all these years. Only one remaining choice for each of us: H.C. opts to leave his bivouac stove behind, and I, my bivouac tent. These items are necessary for others, but not for us, goes our telepathic agreement. Some things seem to never change.

As I bend to secure my bindings, the memory of carrying a full pack on touring skis returns, and I must pay close attention to my balance. Mary, six months pregnant, will wrap herself in a blanket, sit in the sun, and watch us until we ski out of sight. I am confident that she will be fine. These days, I save the Velcro in my life for outdoor gear, so Mary and I have little difficulty saying goodbye, even though this will be our first time apart.

I surprise myself at how focused, how consciously committed I am today. I carry with me an awareness, almost palpable, of my death, but I do not push it away, and so I feel more prepared than ever. It reminds me of the critical moment in a mother's labor when fear fills the space, and the key to having a successful, natural delivery is for her to feel the fear, to acknowledge its immensity; with it, the birth canal opens.

Soon, I am alone and I am with H.C. He is a man of few words, and so the awareness of being alone constantly accompanies me when the two of us travel together.

As he points the way for the route, I override my intuition and agree. This is a dangerous aspect of travelling with such a master: I must not abandon my knowing. A mile later, it is clear that we have erred, but the day is sunny and forgiving, so we cheerily reorient ourselves.

The next test comes quickly, when we begin to climb, and I decide to put synthetic skins on the bottom of my skis. It first appears that I drilled the catch too far down the ski, and I am immediately calling myself a fucking imbecile for my ineptitude, for not having let the experts at the outdoor shop mount them. I get tight, frustrated at my predicament. Then, just before I heave the skins, I see that there is one possible adjustment, and I give it a go. Voila! Not only do they work, but I quickly realize that they will soon stretch, meaning I did a good job after all. My father never let me watch him work on the car or on things mechanical, because he feared that I might like it, just as he did, and that I might decide to live that kind of life, one that he judged against. Still fresh in my mind are his words from our visit last week: "Stu, life is one big sweat."

The trail turns steep and stays that way. As I stop every fifteen yards or so to catch my breath, I reflect that my boys would have found this tough going. The combination of my bronchial condition and a lack of high-altitude preparation have put me in this unusual position. In times past, I would have bounded up this stretch. Today, I feel humbled by the physical challenge. I am a different man than I was on our last hut trip, three years ago, when I still had a reputation for being a "mountain animal." That name was music to my ears back then. These days, my desire to push myself wanes as I listen more respectfully to how my body feels.

We meet a large group of skiers coming down the steep trail; all but two are descending on their butts.

Up or down, this stretch is not especially fun, so I turn to my rich inner life for a meditation. I choose the men of the Tenth Mountain Division. These men have long held a fascination for me, since they represent a bridge for generations, and because of their mystique. My generation despised war, while our parents swallowed it with fatal acceptance, as if it were a requisite pill for existence on the planet. But the Tenth Mountain Division transcended the black and the white. They were not your basic soldiers. No, the Tenth was composed of Ivy Leaguers (the only Americans who could afford to ski at that time), as well as mountain men, Native Americans, wilderness adventurers, artists, muleskinners, cowboys, European skiers and climbers who early on saw what Hitler was about and came here, vagabonds, romantics, poets, and visionaries.

Put them into any other division, and they would be misfits. But they *were* the Tenth. They became lifetime friends. And they did not act like soldiers when they trained in skiing and mountaineering at Camp Hale. They sang songs about their ninety-pound packs (often weighing in at 150 pounds, as compared to mine of sixty, at most) as they linked their stem-christiana turns down the slopes of these mountains. They slept outside in thirty-below wind chill, and joyously prepared morning coffee for each other in their tents prior to heading off into another day. They transcended this valley's campfire smog in the winter and endless mud each spring. They were graced by their love for the mountains, and the mountains gave them what no other soldiers received: the spirit of place, a reverence for nature, and a deep understanding of the power of cooperation.

No division trained harder. When they finally entered combat, attacking a high fortress in the Italian Dolomites, they succeeded where two other divisions had failed, setting the Nazis to route. "Succeed" is a delicate word, one I doubt many of them would use, since 900 gave their lives.

After the war, these legendary figures, the hooded, white-clad soldiers, built a large part of America's ski and outdoor recreation industry, led some of the most formidable mountain ascents of the time, and skied for the Olympic team. They also entered mainstream occupations, such as architecture, where they had great influence with their creative vision and charisma.

Did they know something that I do not? I picture them never complaining, always accepting adversity with good cheer. I compare how quick I often am to pity myself in difficult situations, as I already am on this long climb. I fancied that they had a tap into an endless energy source at that crucial point where other mortals give up. They were, to a good degree, overlooked by our mass culture, but this energy tap, this mystical connection, certifies them as my personal heroes. Today, they are remembered by this magnificent hut and trail system.

The interminable, sweaty ascent ends as we break out of the trees and into the tundra. We stop, take our packs off, and rest on a rock outcropping. While we gaze at the peaks to the south, H.C. relates one of his favorite stories, that of a Frenchman named Maurice Herzog, who led an epic first Himalayan ascent of Annapurna. If it's not me dwelling on these giant figures, it's my partner. Right now, I feel puny out here. Still, I am all ears.

Herzog travelled to the highest mountains in the world in his attempt to reach the summit of Annapurna. As he and his partner neared the top, they both entertained severe frostbite, and his companion asked Herzog what he would do if he turned back. Herzog astonished himself by replying that he, the expedition leader, would go on alone. His partner immediately committed to continue, at which point, Herzog, for the first time free from anxiety, felt abundant energy and saw the mountains of his dreams, a fantastic universe.

"In no time he stood on the summit in a state of ecstasy, having met his life's greatest goal," H.C. tells me.

But their descent just as quickly became a plunge into pain and despair, a hell-world beyond imagining. Herzog was reduced to being comatose and was carried out on the back of a porter, his physical and nervous energies shot.

H.C., seeing that I am appropriately spellbound, continues.

"He lost his will to live and wanted to die, while his extremities were rotting of frostbite. But he came through that deepest night to a new life. And you know, Stu, he went on to become the French Minister of Education," he cheerfully concludes.

The late afternoon sun casts a soft glow upon this high landscape, and the air remains warm, friendly-feeling. We put our packs on and resume the climb. Up here, the snow has softened, creating pockets of junk snow--places where the base caves in--and we frequently find ourselves dropping into hip-deep, heavy snow. Along a high ridge, we search for the saddle from which we will finally orient down to the hut. After a couple of spills, I feel extremely vulnerable in the winter tundra.

Alpenglow spills onto the Mount of the Holy Cross. It is a captivating sight, even now that one arm of the "cross" has eroded away. Surely the soldiers of the Tenth drew great inspiration when it was all intact.

We reach the saddle and see that a fast, hard-packed descent to the hut awaits us.

As we observe the route, H.C. says, "I think today might have been too much for Aaron and Dylan. I mean, this is challenging terrain and it's so easy for something to go wrong out here, and if that happened, it would have been serious."

The run down is a maze of changing snow conditions, and I pride myself on being skilled at this. In fact, it is the only area where I can surpass H.C. His knees gave way a number of years ago, and since he underwent surgery to have cartilage removed, he is almost always conservative on the downhills. Not so in kayaking or technical climbing, where, at age 53, he is stronger than ever. I marvel at his fitness and at his approach to life. He has always met wilderness as an aesthetic, be it in the perfect site that he finds for his tent or in the way that he packs his gear. He displays grace and efficiency in moving through the backcountry. In certain circles, he is a living legend, although I don't think he's ever let that in. His age places him with Yvon Chouinard, Royal Robbins, and all those other legendary clothing manufacturers. I'm too lazy to research how old Ralph Lauren, Calvin Klein, Polo, and those legendary climbers are, so I won't include them. Speaking of his age, had he been born twenty years earlier, I'll bet that he would have been a member of the Tenth.

I am eight years younger than H.C. and have created quite a different reality. I have lots of children, while he has none. His life appears to be much simpler than mine, all the way around. Yet there are similarities. We have both dedicated our lives to service. He runs the community food share program for the county, and to complement it, he obtained a grant for a community garden and greenhouse to provide the elderly with fresh food. I have a healthcare practice. I've also noticed that, like me, he has less time these days for expeditions or for spontaneity; we are both over-committed.

But this night, far from our daily lives, we find ourselves sharing the hut with a group from Rocky Flats nuclear facility, a place the righteous folk from Boulder love to hate. I recall Santa Fe's proximity to the nuclear frontier of Los Alamos, and our constant disdain in those days for that town. I believe that to see the truth of these rarified communities, they mustn't be taken alone. They exist in proximity to the evil factories in the same inseparable manner that yin accompanies yang, as vital components of the same sphere of energy.

Regardless of the politics, the people from Rocky Flats are certainly kind and respectful toward us. It strikes me as odd, though, how they clock each other's bathroom visits to see which sex takes more time (the women are faster, hands down), and that one of them brought a C.B. radio for calling home.

I prepare dinner, simple and whole-grainy. H.C. eats a lot tonight, to his surprise. We really get into the Ak Mak crackers with butter. As I watch him, I observe that had he been responsible for the food, he would have brought as little as possible. I remember kayak trips where he ate granola and oranges--that's all--for close to a week. Food for him is obligatory, and I see a similar attitude in myself. I have forever been reluctant to nourish myself. Somewhere, soft was spelled w-e-a-k. From early on in my life, the threat of turning into an undisciplined fat boy loomed. Tonight, my obsession with the difficult is nearing its end. I have begun to acknowledge my hunger for the gentle and do not so readily judge against it.

Our sleep is fitful as we adjust to a crowded loft, snoring, high altitude, and wicked winds. Even so, I awaken to find my lungs already clearing. But I am conscious of a numbness in the fourth toe of my left foot. It began after a kayak trip seven years ago, when my marriage began to unravel, and I have monitored it carefully. It has come and gone, but not worsened. My father has multiple sclerosis, a condition I've seriously studied. My toe represents the M.S. disposition in me. Each day, however, I come closer to taking the next step, a giant one, in the commitment to my healing. When that dedication is secure, my toe will feel normal.

While we eat breakfast the following morning, a man asks H.C. about his wood Bonna skis. I don't understand what the big deal is--after all, he has only been skiing on the same pair of skis for nearly 25 years, and they are in great condition. During this time, I have trashed my fair share of skis. I remember how H.C. would help me fastidiously fiberglass broken tips back onto my skis. To this day, he never uses skins, standard fare for hut-to-hut expeditions, to climb uphill. Every party we meet along the way from here on out will regard his skis with delight and amusement.

Then there is his ancient Kelty pack, which he has carried all over the world, and is, of course, in fine shape. Why, H.C. has been out here doing these sorts of things forever. I recall him running mountain trails years before there ever was such a sport. He made friends one year with a wild turkey, and the two of them would regularly convene in a meadow where he stopped to nap along the way. He even carried its picture in his wallet.

When the Rocky Flats party departs, I suddenly feel vulnerable in the spacious hut. But as the last of them skis out of sight, a sense of quiet arrives. I play at splitting a little wood and fantasize on teaching my boys the fine points of this art. The reality, however, lies elsewhere. I reflect that like much of what I do, my wood splitting was self-taught and I approach it recklessly. H.C., on the other hand, knows how to split wood. He makes it look like his calling. Oh, but I do declare, I fold my toilet paper.

Synchronicity arises on a table, where *Newsweek* reveals which nuclear facilities hold the most poison. Guess who the winner is? The morning goes like this, as we unwind rather aimlessly. But, something is lurking, awaiting our decision: our choice as to what we will do this afternoon. We planned this as a layover day, a time to rest and to ski free from full packs. We have options today. The most attractive is to ski up to the top of a nearby mountain and then telemark turn forever down a treeless paradise. Or, we could ski out and discover some exotic terrain. A final possibility would be to explore a good part of tomorrow's route, certainly the least exciting option. However, the guidebook has made much ado about the trek, citing difficulty in route-finding, as well as a prominent cornice that becomes dangerous in stormy weather. So far, the skies are clear, but the wind continues.

While H.C. and I discuss the possibilities, we hear a group arrive on snowmobiles. Yuk. But it turns out that they are from the Tenth Mountain Hut Association and are reconnoitering the area to see how close to the huts snowmobiles can come without disturbance, since this is a multiple-use area. They bring news that a storm is indeed on its way, and that it's sure to be a whopper. Our decision has been made for us. Still, some part of me can't help but remember times years ago when forest service rangers would do their best to scare the shit out of H.C. and me with countless horror stories as we prepared for our first descent down some wilderness river.

On our last hut tour we encountered spring-like conditions, and the trails threatened to turn to mud. We were laying over at a hut, and the prospects for magical skiing the next day looked grim indeed. I walked out onto the great deck that night, and observed a starry sky. The weather forecast for the week called for sun and more sun. Suddenly, I felt possessed to do my first snow dance. I really got into it, and called to the proper authorities for a heaping of fresh powder. My good friend and ski partner from Santa Fe scoffed at me and declared that he was going to sleep on the deck, under the stars. He awakened me at midnight with the news that a blizzard had arrived. By morning, it had dumped well over a foot of snow. We later learned that the vicinity we were skiing was the only area where it snowed.

What's happening to me? Here I am telling tales of days gone by.

Today, the promise of snow poses a kind of threat. It is sobering, as we prepare to do our reconnaissance. I have learned to read H.C. from what he does not say, and all morning I sensed his respect for tomorrow's route. He is a master at making others think that they are doing the deciding, all the while relying on the gravity of his substance to speak for him. He usually gets his way.

Most of the afternoon is uneventful, and at times boring, because it takes place on old roads, and because H.C. is the only man I know who makes me appear talkative. The instant I set my skis on a road, my energy drains. For me, they lack the mystery and sensuousness of a narrow, undulating trail. I make the most of it by skiing down through the glades instead, until we reach the bottom of the valley and get confined to the road.

Our route appears to be straight-forward until we reach a large "park" where many trails and old roads converge. We gravitate to a large map, posted on a wooden frame, clearly intended for summer use. It is a critical moment, because, out of habit, we defer to the map as gospel and abandon our intuition, good sense, and ability to read our own map and compass. We find ourselves on a wild goose chase, going round and round under a setting sun, having made a shrine of a goofy map standing in the middle of nowhere. Anxiety begins to set in, because it is somewhere in this "park" that our orienteering adventure will begin, and we have failed to find the starting point. The darkening sky harkens us back to our hut. We ski carrying a sense of failure, along with increasing trepidation about tomorrow.

We arrive at the hut in darkness and are greeted by two women from New York who skied in while we were gone. I quickly feel comfortable with our new hutmates.

As is our custom, I get cleaned up, and H.C. does not. Next, I fix dinner, while he pores over the topographic map. He studies it with his compass, and will persist until he is satisfied that he has solved the riddle. In the meantime, I am careful to distance myself, so as not to rely on him for the solution. I decide that my intuition will pick up tomorrow where I left it today, and after dinner I join H.C. in studying the map, then move close to the woodstove with a cup of tea.

I consider Mary moving into the third trimester, and how I am loving this pregnancy. I have truly felt pregnant, in the sense that I have become quite invisible to the day-to-day process of living, protected as it were, in a kind of sanctuary of creation. For too many years, I have stood on the front lines, dedicated to my healing work and to my kin's survival, but now a change is in progress. I am able to focus on and surrender to the pregnancy as an energetic shift, as a new chapter, as a rebirth. Something is growing inside me, a long-dormant desire to feel happy, a desire to actually live, not simply run from activity to activity. I am only now beginning. The pregnancy is my calling to a different way of being, and at this time I cannot define the changes. I can only listen, feel, and witness my becoming.

On the last hut trip, I was still captive to the ways of unrequited love. I was out of touch with all of my feelings except the grief of my divorce and the separation from my children. I was broken, but I had not yet committed to waking up. More relationship heartbreak would soon remedy that.

Yes, I want to live, since that is what I have come for, and what I have only begun to do. No, I do not need to put my life on the line anymore, even in the wilderness, in order to gain the peak experiences. This, I realize, reflects a big shift. I am walking through a door to a life beyond such extremes. It is a world of non-violence, grounded in the fullness and truth of every moment, and it does not require the imminence of death to stir a bit of life. Inside myself, these days, I catch such glimmers.

Strange: that life-or-death edge has been the place where H.C. and I have usually enacted our relationship. Too, I always carried a slightly hysterical demeanor that revealed itself most in his presence, but that has faded since I began the journey home to all of my feelings.

On this trip, I am aware more than ever that much of his silence reflects a captivity to feelings that he has judged against. He is one of the children of Kennedy, an early member of the Peace Corps. He went to the magical kingdom of Nepal, and worked under the late, legendary mountaineer, Willy Unsoeld, whose life ended suddenly on Mt. Ranier. Upon his return, H.C. married his beautiful dream girl, and that's where the dream broke. His wound is apparent. In fact, it was what I first saw when I met him. A purple heart. I recall that she ended up having M.S. What I know for certain about this disease is that it reflects unexpressed rage, which then transforms into a paralysis of self-opposition and erosion of the will. But the divorce did ultimately clear the path for H.C. to have a deeply compatible marriage.

No, he would not have fit into "The Tenth." He did not choose to be born 20 years sooner because he is too pacific. War is not his way. He is rare, this man. He is always true to his word. He reads Ghandi for inspiration, and he constantly manifests the upright and independent. Still, at times, his extreme independence feels as if it pushes away the possibility for greater intimacy.

Just now, I catch a rare glimpse of H.C. winding down. It is hard for him to do nothing, but he is at it, as I write. Time for me to join him. Goodnight.

During the night, the winds abate, and the storm arrives. Although it is not yet snowing heavily, we are in a cloud, and that lends drama to the day. Our hutmates voice their concern about our journey and encourage us to stay put. I feel sober, quite ready to ski out on an alternate trail, which is a sure bet to get us home safely if we are in over our heads. While I prepare my gear, I read a plaque on the wall dedicating this hut to a man and a woman who were killed climbing. Posterity, I observe, carries its price.

Once we are out the door, the clouds reflect my quietude. Down we go, gliding through a hushed morning. To my surprise, it is H.C. who breaks the silence. From out of nowhere, he relates a story about a time in high school. I listen carefully, sensing a missing piece to the puzzle.

"When I was a senior," he recalls, "it looked as though we might have a really outstanding baseball team."

Now, I remember hearing how H.C. was the ace pitcher for that team.

He continues, telling me how a couple of players got their girlfriends pregnant, married them, and quit the team. As a result, the team became mediocre.

"I was relieved to get through the season," he says. "At that point, I got sick of relying on a team of people to lead you to success. And, success was only about winning. It became empty for me."

That summer he took up climbing with a remarkable man, a professor of philosophy, who emanated a quiet serenity.

"What a dramatic experience that was for me. Although I'd been aware of the mountains, I had never given them much thought."

But under the tutelage of the man who held mountains and Marcus Arelius in great regard, H.C. awakened to his passion.

Thanks to H.C.'s atypical verbosity, we arrive at the "park" in no time. We are accompanied by none of yesterday's apprehension, even though a whiteout appears likely for our ridge crossing. Each of us silently sets off independently in search of the departure point for our ascent. It does not feel like a competition that drives us so much as the need for redemption from yesterday's debacle. And each of us in our own way soon arrives at a blue diamond posted on a tall spruce, sign of the Tenth Mountain trail we've been in search of.

As we approach the crux passage of our trip, I wonder, "What am I doing here?" My sons carry on their lives in a world away from me today. They were my "cause" for this trip, or so I thought. The men of the

Tenth Mountain Division had a cause, a discernible evil to confront. Too, Herzog and his party carried the soul of a dispirited French nation on their climb, in the aftermath of World War II. Their success was a redemption of sorts. But there is nothing substantive here for us to overcome and we have no anthem to spur us on to self-sacrifice. In fact, I am now dedicated to releasing sacrifice as my way. No, it's just H.C., wilderness, and me, as it's always been, with few strings attached.

Since I began coming out here with H.C., my desire has been ultimately to bring it back home, and I am confident, now, that I am on track. As Mary joyously progresses each day toward claiming her true, healthy feminine, I feel free, finally, to move into my pure yang, my healthy masculine, and to feel at home wherever I am. Until now, I had to make pilgrimages to wild regions to taste this freedom.

My need for wilderness adventures is fading. I first ventured out as a young man, starving to discover the freedom of healthy expression, at a time when my every breath reflected opposition. Wilderness journeys introduced me to the fullness of the here and now. No matter how crazy my life is being, embarking on one of these voyages always brings me back to what is real.

So, perhaps I am here to give gratitude for a most important component in my life. Maybe this time I have come unknowingly, embarked once again in this ritual with H.C, to mark the end of the beginning of my journey home.

As we climb above timberline, I sense avalanche danger. I am happy to note that I am fully participating in finding the route, instead of collapsing into an old dependence on H.C. The feeling that I could die here is sobering and helps me to counter the spacy sense that I have in this world of no contrast. For long stretches, I see no trees, and the landscape is without definition. I concentrate on breathing, and on placing one ski in front of the other, which helps counter hovering anxiety. We stop for lunch, but it is too eerie (too windy and too cold as well) to be any fun. The only real difficulty I experience comes after lunch, when I begin to hyperventilate for a moment from coldness. The actual skiing is technically easy.

H.C. brought goggles, and I did not. Without them, I have no depth perception, only a constant wall of white/grey.

From out of the void, H.C. shouts, "Stop, Stu."

This is all the information I need to know that I am skiing perilously close to the cornice.

Ever so slowly, we work our way around an impressive drop-off, to a reasonable route down, and soon we are back in the trees. Now, perception returns, and I delight in telemarking down the riverbed, feeling suddenly much lighter. The snowfall is beautiful as it covers the trees and the mountains. The world turns soft. H.C. complains about the ski tracks that we periodically saw on the ridge before the wind erased them. He wanted more of an orienteering challenge. We would have met the challenge just fine, I feel certain.

But the word from here on out, this full moon day, is most certainly "soft." We arrive at a hut that is privately owned and is therefore different than the standard, rather Spartan, Tenth Mountain huts. Now I must qualify my description of these huts, because they are beautiful, and they are beautifully located. I say "Spartan" in the Zen sense of the word. This is a contrast to what greets us when we enter today's hut, and close the door on the now-heavy snowfall blowing in behind us.

A gigantic antique woodstove, laughing with a roaring fire, holds down the center of the room. Three jolly older folks are sitting around the dining table, a feast laid before them. They greet us with an offer of Turkish apricots, grapes, cheese, crackers, and schnapps. It's as if they've been waiting for us. They carry a contagious levity, and I feel like a child coming to stay at my favorite grandparent's house.

After we enjoy the food and company, we explore the hut and choose a cathedral-ceilinged bedroom, with actual beds, for the night. No dormitory is this. H.C. is loving the place. It even has hot and cold running water.

Sam, Jean, and Elka, our new friends, act as our hosts, so we kick back and soak in the magic.

Later, the sky clears, and we venture out for a full moon tour. Once was a time when H.C. and I would make such tours under the influence of some mind-expanding substance. We took hallucinogens seriously and rarely. Tonight, we could not ask for more, as he and Elka zoom out for some real exercise.

I choose to move more slowly. I stop among a family of great, beautiful spruce. I feel the trees being concerned for me. In comes the memory of a woman I love, a woman who cannot see the soul of hers that I so deeply love. I feel the loss, but I do not dwell. She is off to India, in search of that soul. (What kept calling me to more wilderness journeys was the search for mine.) At the time of the last hut trip, we were living together as starstruck lovers, still ignorant of the ways of love. I returned from the trip more determined than ever to make it work. Now, I understand that either it is or it is not.

Secure in my aloneness, I ski back to the hut.

On the final morning, I awaken to clouds the color and shape of salmon swimming in the sky above the Holy Cross Range. Last night, I dreamed an exquisite dream about my anima, about being happily and deeply in love with a woman who was perfect for me. I then came home and told Mary about her, that she was perfect for me, and that she was inside me.

I observe our room and see my clothes in disarray, relative to H.C.'s. On my side, crumpled Kleenex lines the windowsill. I contract in self-judgment. I look again, and this time see it as one of my boys' bedrooms. I grin and feel my body soften.

After a relaxed breakfast, we bid a fond farewell to our fairy godparents. The sky is cobalt blue, the day warm, and the fresh snow sparkles the colors of millions of diamonds. It has taken me until now to make peace with my pack. The way is soft and sensual. I glide down, floating on a cloud of powder, flowing from one turn into the next, effortlessly engaged in movement without beginning and without end.

Around a bend, we startle three pure white ptarmigans and stop for a moment to delight in them. H.C. continues on. As I watch him, I notice that I no longer feel a "kid" in his presence. I am also more at peace with his stoicism. I recognize his limitations, but I do not long for him to be different. How ironic, the change I've observed in him during this journey. Each day, he's grown looser and more at ease.

Too soon, we arrive at H.C.'s truck. I realize with a kind of melancholy that when I return home to Mary for the final trimester, none of my children will be living with us.

During the ride home, my attention is grabbed by a semi bearing the name "Covenant Transport." I am instantly reminded that I am releasing a legacy, the agreement field upon which we created this civilization and to which we have all made ourselves subject. The covenant between God and Abraham called for sacrifice, the way of the scientific-material search. The way of separation. The way of nation-states. The way of war. The hook was posterity and possessions.

We pass the semi.

I am filled with gratitude for these adventures and especially to H.C., for his teaching and for our friendship. These times have given me the inspiration to carry on, the courage to begin to break free, and have helped provide me with windows on a possible life, a new covenant.

Spring Breaks

March 20, 1994, at the waning tide of the material-scientific civilization. Mary and I are driving down to southern Colorado to pick up my two youngest boys, Kai and Mikael, for spring vacation. The ride has been a struggle through inclement weather. I finally surrender to fatigue, and retire to the back seat for a rest.

I sink into muddy musings regarding where my life is going. Of late, my acupuncture work is increasingly draining, and I must hold on toward the end of each treatment day. I have devoted fifteen years to mastering my work, making it my bread and butter. Yet now, I deeply sense that my days with it are numbered. I have even come to question the future of one-on-one healing practice: the closer I come to my full personal healing, the more clearly I see how so many hands-on practitioners are bringing blind rage into the arena and are actually governed by it. We live in a time of fakirs, those who prosper in times of desperation.

As I lay back, and Mary steers us over a storm on La Vita (the life) Pass, I sink into an altered state. At some point, the elders, Hopi men, surround me. Although they do not materialize, I immediately recognize them. I ask them, "where to from here?" and they reply that in order for me to be prepared for the life that I am approaching, one step remains. That step is not about my doing anything, but is rather a receiving of all of who I already am, accepting what this life most certainly is. The image is of a glove, made for me, and what remains is for me to put my hand into it, to claim this. They are solemn, and they are certain, both of their message and of my readiness.

This encounter takes place under Blanca Peak, one of the four sacred peaks of the Southwest, just as Mary's meeting months earlier with the women elders took place under the San Francisco Peaks. The meeting feels perfectly natural, and once their message is transmitted, they are gone.

The experience is the most recent in a series of preparations, of an ongoing transmission since we discovered that we were pregnant, seven months ago. We've had the sense of being in a kiva, an underground ceremonial chamber, common to the Hopi people, and have felt virtually invisible to the outside world. The

Hopi attribute the kiva to the life source, the mother, and consider it the place we emerged from.

We have had other meetings with kachinas, as well. The kachinas represent the Hopi's link between the world of no-form, or apriori, and material reality, the aposteriori realm. So although today's visit is out of the ordinary, I am not surprised. Also, whenever the transmissions have occurred, we've never felt afraid, even though we do not "understand" why the Hopi, or, for that matter, why us.

Although Mary and I both received our messages in the Southwest, we feel certain that our work lies elsewhere, in a realm that is more empty, spiritually younger, a place open to a unique creation. And our initiation has taught us that family is the primary vehicle for transformation.

Almost as quickly as I reorient and collect myself, we arrive in Alamosa, meeting the boys and their mother for a parent "switch." My pain upon seeing Bobbie and my children is so immediate and so great, that even Mary, I would later learn, could feel it and wondered why the split had to happen.

It is raining here, darkening by the moment, as we load the guys and their gear, exchanging awkward cordialities with Bobbie. Sophie, the family dog from my former life, softens the meeting with her great and unconditional love as she jumps all over me and kisses me.

Finally, the boys are alone with us, and we take off, heading north up the San Luis Valley. Soon the light turns golden, bathing the trees and the peaks in the glow of the equinox, which occurred the moment we rendezvoused with the boys. We are travelling to the area between Aspen and Glenwood Springs because it is the place where our hearts soar, and, coincidentally, where some land has become available for us to look at this week. How fortuitous that the boys will get to see it, too.

Mikael asks what the plan is for the next day, and I say that I am taking Kai skiing, and that he and Mary are going swimming. I do not even ask him to join us skiing, given his control drama with it over these years; how many times was everyone ready to go skiing when Mikael would suddenly declare that he hated to ski, that he wasn't going? Of course, I would then stay back with him.

But today, his response is immediate, "Can I ski with you guys?"

I reply, free of any investment in the outcome, that he is welcome to. His desire does not feel compulsive to me. Instead, I sense that it is arising formatively, as a new agreement, free from the roles that we formerly played.

The drive, which has historically seemed long, flows effortlessly along a carpet of light, although Kai keeps bringing up a premonition of something wierd, maybe bad. We tell him to honor it, and that it will not be bad as long as he stays in touch with it.

As we drive through Glenwood Canyon and gawk at the rising water on the Colorado River, Kai says that he wants me to teach him how to kayak. Am I hearing things? My dreams about life with my children, long ago shattered, then released, are surfacing in a new way. I see myself in a different light, no longer as simply the overburdened provider, the sacrifice for my kin. Today, the dream is becoming our dream, and my life begins to carry a collective quality. The drive has been easy, and I feel less burdened by the mile. Something special is unfolding.

We stop for dinner at a Chinese restaurant, and Kai's fortune reads, "Unusual experience will enrich your life." He comments that something is definitely up, and in the days ahead, he will observe that he feels altered. Using his body's size for the descriptive, he says that he feels bigger here.

Mikael's fortune reads, "Positive attitude will bring desired result." The week will verify this. Mary gets her usual health, happiness, and prosperity readout. My fortune reads, "Be true and trust each other and all will be well." This one flies right by me.

From the instant we arrive at the vacation cabin, the guys love it, call it heaven, and exclaim how they feel different. Mikael says that he is no city boy. They love the loft. I dream deep dreams.

The dreams carry a common strand: I have arrived, both in my writing and in my medicine. I realize this, because in the medicine dream, people are asking me to address a national meeting to teach them about my work. They want my essence, and they want it for nothing in exchange. In another dream, writers are approaching me as I lecture at a writers' workshop, asking me to include their work in my next book. I grasp that my writing has been seen, and that they want to ride the wave. Again, they want my essence, for nothing, to pull me and to exploit me. For me, the dreams are only reflections of my sense of self-worth. What is it here that I cannot see?

In the morning, the boys and I head for Snowmass and a day of skiing, while Mary stays back at the cabin. Mikael, a novice, channels his endless energy into the desire to learn to ski, to have a breakthrough, and today, he is nothing short of remarkable. By mid-afternoon, he is skiing through the trees with us, and loving it.

The boys and I transform into three friends, locked into a special place on a perfect spring skiing day. The sky is the soft powder blue of the Elk range, and the air temperature is balmy. To the south of this range, there is less moisture, and the sky turns more cobalt; the world takes on a sharper edge. To the north, there is too little contrast between mountain and sky for my taste. I have found that it is here, in these mountains, where I best harmonize with the world. The slopes become our song.

On our last run, we take it all the way from the top, weaving in among the trees and sinking into deep powder, until we reach some steep and extremely bumpy stuff on a remote part of the mountain. Kai and I agree to meet at the bottom of a gully, some two hundred yards down, then traverse the remaining descent together. I stay close to Mikael, as I feel concerned about not getting him into terrain that is so difficult as to dim his enthusiasm, as to scare him, especially this late in the day, especially this volatile Taurus child of mine. Our relationship runs deep, grounded in his premature exit-- fourteen weeks early--from his mother's womb. The echo of a critical care doctor's words forever accompany me. Only hours after he was born, we were looking down at him, hooked into artificial breathing equipment and loads of other wires, when the doctor said, "This guy could turn out to be a rosebud."

What he did not add but what was understood, was, "If he lives." But as he uttered those words, my newborn was looking at me, all three pounds of him, transmitting his great life will, telling me that there was no doubt that he had come to be here, blasting his message directly to my heart, over, around, and through all the technological apparatus.

Shadows grow longer, air temperature drops. I seek an easier route down to Kai and the gully. Too late, I realize that the gully itself, not the mountainside, is where the easier skiing lies. Mikael is unfazed, although he is falling a good bit, losing skis often in the process. I begin to call Kai, but receive no answer. I start feeling as if I have violated some safety code, led my children too deeply into danger. I holler louder and more frantically for Kai. We have no contingency plan for getting separated, and now I am blaming myself full bore. I see that Mikael and I could climb a ridge, over to the next valley and considerably easier skiing, so I offer it to him.

"No thanks, Dad. This is where we skied to, and I want to finish it."

In this moment, just as my trepidation about our predicament peaks, gone is an old agreement between father and son. He is soon to turn twelve and has remained every bit my baby during the entire time, for better and for worse. But a new child, a baby, is due soon, and that reality is ushering in a beautiful change today. I am now skiing beside my son, who has chosen to embrace a passion of mine as his own, and is not balking at the challenge. Today he is stepping into a new role.

We ski slowly, as I lead the way, still worrying about Kai. A ski patrolman arrives, sweeping the slopes at day's end. He helps Mikael out, too, and is astounded to learn that this is only his second day on skis. Soon, we converge upon other patrolmen at the end of the gully. They escort us to the bottom, more joining us at each trail confluence, just as the Texas Rangers, at the end of that old T.V. show, would magically multiply into a formidable triangular configuration. At some juncture, I tell Mikael to follow me and to stop wedging his skis, since it takes too much effort. He doesn't miss a beat, and soon we are paralleling effortlessly to the bottom, with the huge contingent of patrolmen behind us, down to Kai, waiting in consternation.

Upon our return to the cabin, we learn that Mary's day has been slow and restful. I bring in an edge, a defensive posture honed from my history with insatiable, insecure partners who made me pay after I spent time with others in my life, even my children. Mary barely gives it notice, because it belongs, after all, to me. The boys don't miss a beat, and continue to blend with Mary as if they've been together forever.

After a fun dinner, Mikael retires with a scary book, Kai stakes out the loft for the night, Mary is quickly into deep pregnancy sleep, and I observe everyone in the tiny cabin feeling secure, and with that, filled with love. I sink into sleep, feeling delighted to be a part of this world.

The next day is look-at-the-land day. This particular land is not even on the frenzied market yet. It called us. We will be the first to see it, ahead of the hordes of Californians and Southerners escaping the violent collapse of their worlds. The land is located on the banks of a beautiful river, one of my kayaking favorites from long ago. I approach without expectation. After the last time we bid on some nearby land, and it was not accepted, I felt crushed, but something has been telling me that this place is it. We procure an instrument for determining passive solar potential, then drive to meet our real estate agent and one of the owners at the top of the dirt road.

Along the way in my life, as I have come closer to realizing my fullness, I have pieced together the puzzle of my dream home, a place that has it all, the ingredients necessary for my kin and me to reach full wingspan. It is a place where I see my family happily living, no compromise, heaven on earth. Simple. It will be a place where the power of nature is so strong that our minds cannot possibly lead us astray, where I will joyously defer and let a greater force guide the craft, while I am free to sink into every moment.

It will be a home that holds the magic of my wilderness journeys: unpredictable, increasingly alive each day, quiet, yet filled with the dynamic of each moment, spontaneous, life being lived on a delicious yet fully responsible edge. A place where competitive ego desire gives way to consensus, where we constantly clarify and refine our souls' purpose, where we walk in beauty and in balance. A place that brings the outside in, so as to every moment remember where we are and who we are. A place to play, to rest deeply, and to constantly realize, practice, and be reminded of our creative intention, an ongoing meditation on awakening. A place where working together is as effortless as playing together. A place for children of all ages to release the past and the future, in surrender to the aliveness of place. Where there is always room for extended family and our family of friends. A seamless sort of place, where all activity is related, overlapping, not compartmentalized, with a living space to reflect this. A constantly challenging yet simultaneously healing environment. With a river running by, to infuse us with the inescapable dynamic of constant change. A place proximal, not distal, to superb wilderness. And, of course, near healing hot springs. A place surrounded on every side by the most beautiful aspects of the American West, spectacular at every season, a place suited for a deep solar home, an energy-independent earthship, yet at an altitude high enough to attract the great birds of the realm. A place with no roads in sight, but easily accessible to culture, civilized needs, and to whatever work we might be doing. A place in a region holding the potential for the next step in our work, however that might manifest. In a community receptive to change and to creativity. Not too cold for gardening, but never too hot, with at least five months of moraine and mountain wildflowers. Great stands of aspen in easy sight, snowcapped sacred peaks to the directions, as well as waterfalls. Great vertical walls of red rock. Amidst a realm that is powerful yet soft. Where bears, mountain lion, and bighorn sheep reside. A place where magic and miracles are welcome. I'm not asking for much.

So, what happens when we actually step into this place? Mary and the boys immediately go to work/play by simply loving the land, while I get tight. Can the electricity line behind us be buried? How attached are the only visible neighbors to their mercury vapor light? Can we upgrade the dilapidated trail down to the river? And what about moving the trailer and the sheds, and clearing the pile of sawdust, that presently occupy my dream site?

Little matter that the owners spent years finding the perfect sight for a solar home in the mountains, that they revere the the land and all of its inhabitants. I skip some rocks with the guys and feel in awe of the setting, but I do not feel high as I did with the land that we did not get, three months ago. And that land could not meet my dreams. Mary did not feel the way I did at the other spot; rather, she felt that it was incomplete, and so she saw it as a compromise.

Not until we are off the land do I realize that my joints are tightening: I am feeling more frustrated by the moment. Mary is tired, in need of a pregnancy nap, and the boys are happy, feeling filled by the land, simply repeating over and over how much they love it and asking me if we are going to get it.

We return to the cabin to pick up bathing suits since we planned to go swimming this afternoon. But there are pressing matters in the space, and Mary and I both know it. The boys would be happy playing around the cabin, and we could hold each other. Mary could rest, and I could search and release my anger. But I am not in touch with what is troubling me. We have chosen to go numb, and so our robot-selves prepare our gear for the next event on the schedule.

Sometime later, I will see that my anger had been the reflection of my not letting myself feel my dream place. I was afraid to have the bliss, so I looked for what was wrong. I chose to keep myself apart from my heart's desire, to remain in the diaspora of separation, and as a result I turned frustrated and furious. At the very moment that I stepped into my dream, I chose negativity and victimization--home sweet home.

At each new moon, I set an intention for the lunar cycle, and two weeks ago, I made the following intention: "To accept gratefully, graciously and gracefully all that I have worked for. To be able to fully and freely accept my family and myself. To immerse myself in the fullness and infinitude that each moment provides me."

These intentions are not creations of a clever mind. They emerge spontaneously when I am prepared to grasp them, and serve as reminders of my priorities, as highway signs. Usually, the setbacks are my best teachers. Once I make the intention, the wheels set in motion, in a most remarkable manner.

The fascinating part about the realm of intentions is that once override occurs, a turn is taken, creating a momentum with a life of its own, providing whatever lessons are called for in order for the heart/mind to get back on course. All of an appropriate magnitude.

Back on the road to the swimming pool, Kai tells us that his unsettling feeling has returned. And I had thought that our final ski run yesterday was what he had been feeling. When Kai addresses such matters, I listen. Born on the total eclipse of the sun, I used to ask him to serve as my personal radar detector on speedy highway jaunts. He was never wrong. As he put it when he was a child, "My knower knows, Dad."

Spring break has attracted lots of families from all over. We are in the pool, having a big time seeing how long we can keep an oversized beach ball in the air. Slowly but surely, more and more children join in our play. I step back and see that our family is charismatic, reflecting brightly in the late afternoon sun, a circle of positively magnetic energy, as a simple game captivates us and fills us with laughter. Kids looking for family and home are drawn to this circle. And it is here that I finally feel the land, our home. I experience the truth of where we stood in the morning, with all of its promise. My heart surges, as the sunlight of reality breaks through the cloudy dreamscape.

Then, almost immediately, I again let my mind have its way, as we elect to continue on our consumption path, rather than slow down and digest the lessons of the day. An old friend has invited us to meet him and his wife for dinner in Aspen, and the boys are hot to rub elbows with the glitterati. No reflection on me, of course. It will mean a bunch of extra miles and socializing, but my mind says it's time to celebrate our "find," and what better place to put an exclamation mark on our new life than Aspen?

Giddiness fills the van as the boys formulate a strategy for the big night ahead, and I savor meeting Aspen on new terms. Long gone are the days when mere proximity to the place filled me with rage, when

Aspen represented the grossest materiality as well as a certain style that I so envied, when I felt great shame for who I was, for being shortchanged by God, when, after every time spent there, I felt too inadequate to face another day. A town filled with beautiful, physically-gifted young people, a level that I could never attain. I hated it, and I hated myself more after each encounter.

Tonight, a triumphant return, after years of hard work, of refining my gifts for this life. Tonight, as we wheel toward Aspen, I stand securely among the foremost healing practitioners in the country, and to say otherwise would be false. Tonight, I travel in alignment with my partner, a beautiful woman who is my match for the times ahead, and I revel in where we are going. As we hit the city limits, endorphins are rocking through my system, and Mary and I squeeze one another's hand. We hold on for the ride.

Soon, we are being carried along toward a restaurant that our friends have suggested. The boys are swept up in the crowdedness and high energy that spring break has created, as well as by the uniqueness of the place. We eat in a regular-looking restaurant, but the food has been elevated to world-class, and it is fun, so rare for us, to partake. Then, we hit a bookstore-cafe for dessert.

The boys muse at interesting books, mostly funny ones, while the rest of us engage in adult conversation. We share our current dreams and catch up on each others' lives at an antique dining table, before a roaring fire, with Mozart playing at a respectful level. When my friend proudly praises my healing capacity, I feel my energy swell. I notice that an attractive woman sitting near us has tapped into my surge, is carefully listening to my friend's words, and that she is staring at me. Her husband notices, too. I bask in the attention, until we walk out, and I see him glaring at me.

A fun night has flown by, and now Mary and I are tired, with miles to go before we sleep, so we hug our friends goodnight. But, the guys are hungry to see Planet Hollywood and the Hard Rock Cafe, and they shift into a pleading, life-or-death mode. I succumb to a compromise, to let them check out Planet Hollywood. To get there, I must backtrack, and as I pull out of an alley, a young woman comes running out of the darkness, and I hit the brakes just inches from her. Suddenly, a giant gust of wind carries in a blizzard of snow, and I tell the boys to hurry up, while Mary and I sit in wait, happy and weary, albeit uneasy from the omens we have just witnessed, under a brightly-lit window sporting the very coat that Schwarzenegger wore in "Terminator 2."

When the boys return, they have stars in their eyes, and Mikael swears that he saw one or two. Snow and rain punctuate the journey home, as Kai and I sit in front, and Mary and Mikael sleep in back. The highway reveals that I am on override, that sleepiness is accompanying us, even though I enjoy hearing Kai talk about our time here. I search the radio for music to pick me up. The road is soaking wet, the night dark, and I yearn for the cabin and bed. I push on, and the ride goes more slowly as the rain falls harder.

The impact occurs in one sudden, yet interminable instant: I hit the brakes, pump them through the skid, then helplessly feel the van slide into the huge deer, on the front passenger side, once, then glance against it again. That sickening sound of metal against life. Astounded, I see the deer continue to run across the highway and out of sight, followed by its family.

I keep driving, absorbed in shock and self-pity. Kai demands that we go back and see if we can find the deer. I obey, turning the van around and straining to see through the driving rain. We get out and search. I sicken at the sight of coarse hairs plastered on the bumper, then give thanks for the plastic car body that gave way upon impact. Each moment I expect to see the corpse, but there is no deer to be seen, and it appears that it even jumped a fence.

Once back on the highway, Mary and the boys try to soothe me, to tell me that there was no way to avoid it, that it came out of nowhere. Perhaps, but I have always found deer to be mystical, serene, deeply feminine, and now my nervous system reverberates the collision. I know that my attitude, and my choices along the way today and tonight, led to the violence. I do not hide how awful I feel, and everyone else expresses their pain and their hopes that the deer is all right. I am in agony and I seek nothing to buffer it. Allowing my pain its full expression is a relatively new posture for me. When I still lived with the boys' mother, I would have pushed the pain away out of a belief that there was no room for vulnerability, and that "negative" emotions such as anger were spiritually primitive on my gallop toward transcendence. I lived my life according to ideas, not the reality of my feelings.

On this long night, I listen to the boys and Mary sleep. I hear Kai retreat into asthma. His condition began about eight years ago, a signal that my marriage was dying, our family ending. These years, it is sporadic. I believe that he is laboring tonight because Mary and I relinquished our responsibility, because we did not respond to our feelings, which caused the boys to become insecure. Some years ago, a person with psychic tendencies volunteered that in a past life Kai was my son, and that one night a fire was consuming our house. He called and called for me, as flames began to consume his room, but I was already dead.

The next morning, we leave the cabin solemnly, and the ride back home is, for me, one of reaction and wariness, of having my shield on constant alert.

We arrive home in the afternoon, and everyone immediately goes their separate ways. I prepare a birthday dinner for Mary, which coincides with a "rehearsal dinner" with our midwives and with the people who we have invited to attend the home birth. Meanwhile, the boys go in search of entertainment and begin to show the frustration of not having any local friends.

I move from chore to chore in shock, still processing the collision, and alongside of it carrying pictures of a possible life with Mary and the children, pictures from a window that opened over the recent days. I see a life of consensus, a life of levity; simple, bright, spontaneous, happy, constantly free to pursue our fullness. A life that honors, without judgment, the reality of each exceptional, multi-dimensional moment.

I practice a form of acupuncture that is based upon the flow of energy through a person's body via channels called meridians, of which there are twenty. The meridians carry the flow of our multi-dimensional being in an uninterrupted manner from one into another, a circle without beginning and without end. So, there is, in reality, only one meridian in each person's body.

In the same way, a family can be seen as one continuous meridian, comprised of individual energy flows. Mary's and my relationship, and our pregnancy, has revealed to me that when two people walk in alignment, that is when they meet in a field of multi-dimensional agreement and without compromise, free from competition, they increasingly become one, and the feeling is not frightening. Rather, it is an exhilarating experience because the relationship is less tedious and allows a freedom to simply be, while standing securely in the growing freedom that the truth provides. Instead of constantly explaining ourselves through misunderstanding, and struggling in the push-pull of power struggle and survival, our communication flows, and we work together. Gone is the realm of mistrust and underlying fear. Our relationship reflects an energy gain, as opposed to an energy drain.

I see that for part of our time on the trip, we and the boys entered into a domain of consensus, that we were living as one meridian and, amazingly, that everyone was getting far more than they needed, that we had become a synergy, an energy much greater than the sum of our parts. Light has begun to be shed on family.

The dinner goes well, with all of my children and some special friends in attendance, but even as I say "well," I mean that it works logistically. I prepare the food from a place of pushing, of feeling over-extended, and everything becomes too mechanical from this vantage point. But familiar.

Slowly but surely the rest of the week with the boys is played out in muting intimacy, of returning to our individual personas. This time I have something to compare it to, and each day feels increasingly fractured and less alive.

By midafternoon of the one day that I spend at work, I realize that I am bored. My mind is instantly off, looking for an old fix. Ever since the divorce, my tonic for emptiness has been romance. But, since Mary and I have been together, fantasizing a romantic fix, such as "I want to marry that woman," or visualizing lovemaking mirrors back to me instantly as phenomenal fantasy, and rings hollow through and through. The reflection is that we are not about filling anything, that we are already full and fully empty, and that the boredom is simply calling me to my calm and to nourishing my center, by experiencing the fullness of my *being*. The trick is to breathe and to accept each moment. But still, I do yearn to be married, to Mary and to my children, to my family, as a part of the energetic that I experienced earlier in the week. For me, this is where life beyond separation begins.

On the guys' final night with us, we travel to my parents' home for a traditional Passover Seder. It could well be the last time that we will all sit together at this ceremony, as my folks are racing against the avalanche of many chronic and acute ailments.

The night is snowy, and since Dylan has over-scheduled, we bring two cars, so that he might leave early. Mary and I drive together, and for the first time, share our wonder at our time in the river valley. I find that, of course, she too has been looking through the window that previewed our possible future. We two are always traveling the same path, encountering virtually identical challenges, regardless of the form they take at the time, or we are seeing the other's challenge from a standpoint of supportive clarity and healthy detachment.

Tonight's dangerous road harkens our nervous systems back to the night of the collision. I tell Mary, "When we were in Aspen, I wasn't loving myself, I was loving my persona."

"Yes," she replies, "We didn't have all our dimensional oars in the water that day. That won't work for us, because we are being called to act from the full upright."

My attraction to Aspen is energetic; that is, it is a center of high energy, and my work is about balancing energy. But, for transformative work to occur, I must be detached. I came to Aspen that night with a swelled head, and I pushed away my feelings to get there. The result was violence.

So, the wound of our collision remains, as my teacher, as a reminder to help me prepare for our time ahead, to help me move uncompromisingly to myself, in order to meet the world and my work in a healthy, unencumbered manner. Homework between now and then. I give thanks to the deer for the sacrifice.

The Seder always occurs at the full moon of spring, and it is the story of the redemption of the children of Israel, of my ancestors' stepping into freedom from slavery. My brother has followed the path of deep orthodoxy and, as usual, tonight he leads the ceremony. Everyone takes turns reading from the story, while he fills in with fascinating commentaries. Just before we begin the ritual meal, which has been reenacted in Jewish homes every year for over five thousand years, he tells of how the first two great redemptions in Jewish history were brought about by persons whose first initials form the word "mother." He adds that the redemption of the future, the final redemption, will be brought about by the prophet Elijah and by the messiah, whose first Hebrew initials also form the word "mother."

Tonight, as we reenact this ceremony, symbol has begun to come alive. Tonight, revolution is in the air, inside each and every one of us, consciously or not. True revolution has little to do with violence; rather, it is an emergence, a movement from darkness into light, an energetic birthing.

The journey home has begun. Regardless of the obstacles, of the demons who tell me to turn back, Mary and I are now on an epic journey. My intention, unconditionally, is to go, to manifest my truth every moment with my words, which well up and reach expression at my medulla, at the confluence with my birth mark, where my head meets the rest of my body-- an important confluence. As the veils drop, my eyes begin to open.

I savor this night, with my children drawn around my parents. My mother and my aunt, her sister, in turn proudly observe the boys. Present, but not yet manifested, is their newest sibling.

Then, Dylan pushes dinner down, and is off to a "Rave," an all-night dance at a secret warehouse rendezvous. After we say goodnight to my family, the rest of us drive home together, on a night when worlds so clearly overlap. In acknowledging this overlap, my journey feels infinitely more full.

Deliverance from external slavery to a tyranny of the mind. Next, deliverance from a tyranny of the mind to . . .

Kahlieh Is Born

April 15. Today, at the moment of truth in a world called income tax, what had appeared to be good, sound fiscal responsibility suddenly became a disaster. I had been picturing Mr. H. and R. Block proudly shaking my hand, with me all smiles. The turnaround happened so quickly.

Only two weeks ago, we scraped together a deposit on our dream land. We then sailed toward tax time, which turned unexpectedly grim when our accountant (not Mr. Block) told us that we had seriously underestimated last year's earnings. Concurrently, many of my acupuncture patients suddenly want to strike deals on their treatment payments.

The noose is being squeezed, and I contract with every bill that I pay. To top it off, we have a baby coming any day.

The timing for money woes turns all the more bizarre when I consider how I feel about my work. At similar moments in the past, I mounted my steed and willed myself to work harder, to call in more patients, to go on override, to go numb, but to meet the challenge, to "just do it." This time, I've kept in touch, and each treatment day, the message comes in more resounding: my passion for engaging in the one-to-one healing, which I've dedicated my life to perfecting, is spent.

It was only a month ago that my diagnostic skills came up to par with the rest of my abilities. In diagnosis, a wall had remained, where I stubbornly persisted in trying to figure out health conditions, instead of practicing pulse reading from the void. The breakthrough came because our pregnancy has been about releasing opposition. When I carried this into my work, a shift occurred. I moved from activity to receptivity. In embracing my yin, I could let go of my mind's desire to be clever and instead allow some space in the treatment room. I became a better listener. At last, I was clicking on all cylinders.

But with the final piece, my remaining spark went. The challenge was gone. So where to from here?

At the core of our healing lies our fullness, a space filled with the light and complete acceptance of who we've always been. The ultimate work of healing is to get from here to there (or from there to here).

In reality, however, I now see that I've participated in various degrees of compromise with my patients. Such agreements protect and perpetuate lies by creating worlds of delusion; they keep us in the death spiral that has been our legacy and that is now accelerating. Over these years I continued to modify my work, but at the core, it remained the same. The endpoint of this agreement is more of the violence of life lived in separation. In short, my treatment room remains, by agreement, a killing ground, fear-based and sacrificial. I attained a certain degree of mastery within that realm, but that achievement has only led to a detachment from which I can see the limits of the paradigm. I want to live a different paradigm.

And so, as the time of our baby's birth approaches, I find us with no money and having little passion left for my proven way of making a living. Our hearts are calling us onward, to a different place, to a place beyond reason. Not impulsively are we going, since the call that we are answering is the call to come home, and the geographic shift is only symbolic of a deeper shift inside, to a way of being, to a place beyond survival, beyond reaction, beyond competition.

April 19. As the trauma of income tax fades, word comes of April 23 being an auspicious day. The grand union of Sirius A and Sirius B will occur, and with it will come our capacity to hold more information, to upgrade--more RAM for our souls, as it were--for the coming times. This alignment, one of my patients tells me, last occurred 90,000 years ago, when the continent of Mu arose. April 23 is also the most auspicious day of each year in several circles, including the realm of Life Medicine. My teacher observed it as the day for giving gratitude to our ancestors, both physical and spiritual. It will be Green Day in England and the day that Earth Day is celebrated in many places here. And, as if that were not enough, it is my former wife's birthday.

Just before dusk, I look up from the dining room table, having felt a presence. Circling over our deck is a golden eagle. The time has come for it to make contact. These past days, I have felt the eagle hovering above the house, but it would disappear as quickly as I appeared outside.

April 20. Two eastern bluebirds arrive, and stay.

April 21. We observe two great blue herons circling overhead, on a day that finds both of us furiously nesting. For my part, I apply stain to the cradle and clean the house.

April 22. Friends from far and wide call throughout the day to check in on the pregnancy. A rainbow appears 72 hours after I made contact with the eagle. Mary and I take a walk at sunset, on a nearby trail, choreographed to the writing on the wall--the imminence of her labor.

Evening falls, and shortly after Richard Nixon is pronounced dead, Mary's water breaks. I light candles, then simply watch her and support her with delight. The labor for her is sensual, a time of celebration and ceremony, not official, but pure and in the moment. She is walking her talk of the last nine months, steeped in her surrender to the contractions, in her commitment to being present. The pain, then, is not what she would call pain: "It is something else, an extraordinary and unique sensation," she simultaneously laughs and cries.

She brings all of her breathing and relaxation to the labor. She is in ecstasy, and I sense her dilating with no problem. Our desire to have this baby at home is great, but there is blood in the amniotic fluid that continues to seep out with each contraction. I call our primary midwife, who is at first reluctant to get out of bed. I assure her that I am familiar with real labor, and that we need her. Word of the bleeding sends her on her way.

Both midwives soon arrive, and the bleeding does not abate. We are uncertain if the blood is coming from the baby or from Mary. The midwives, at this moment, seem more invested in the home birth than we are, and it is finally Mary who expresses an urgency to proceed to the hospital. For me, this is the appropriate time and place on the pyramid of health care for modern medicine, and my feeling body concurs.

Still, our drive to the hospital is shocking because we are entering a world that carries the memory of bright lights, cold steel, invasive procedures, and, ultimately, of cutting. The only consolation, the only real "message" that Mary and I each get is to let go, and so we surrender to the inevitable. And the more we let go, the more something very special unfolds. We are greeted by care and concern, by respect for who we are and for the road we have travelled. We are surrounded by angels.

The doctor examines Mary and diagnoses an abrupted placenta, which means the baby's food supply is being threatened. Despite good heart tones from the baby, we choose a C-section rather than risk endangering or even losing the child.

I decide to watch the Caesarian and am again astonished by Mary's clarity, by her commitment to a healthy baby and to herself.

In the early morning of April 23, I am completely surprised to see the doctor pulling a *boy* out of Mary's belly! He is awake and he is present, from the get go.

Our glowing newborn doesn't appear surprised to emerge at a hospital. He looks great except for black and blue marks on his head. It appears that with a dwindling food supply, he was fighting to get out. I stay with him, while Mary is taken to recovery. Our midwives are with us too, unhesitatingly present and committed to this passage.

Once we knew that we were headed for the hospital, I placed a few calls to loved ones. Curiously, the only one of my children to show up is my eldest, Aaron. I say curious, because I did not show up for his birth, or for that matter, for the first sixteen years of his life. He is immediately taken by how big and strong the baby is. Aaron's support and the midwives' ongoing vigilance frees me to move back and forth between Mary and Kahlieh.

Without blinking, the night metamorphoses into morning. In the course of the march toward daylight, voices begin to accompany me, and they proliferate as I succumb to stress and fatigue. The hand of guilt is squeezing me by the collar for not showing up for Aaron. There is no explanation, no excuse, no forgiveness. I am a bad person.

When we are told that Mary has a fibroid tumor on her uterus, my demons seize the opportunity instantly. They remind me that my ex-wife had a fibroid too, and that it led to Mikael coming fourteen weeks early. I am responsible for this, the voices say, since I failed to diagnosis it during pregnancy, and so did not cure it. Me, the great healer. Furthermore, since I believe fibroids arise from jammed emotions, I recognize now that I tyrannized both of these women into less-than-perfect births.

Why, I ask, can't I be a part of a happy home delivery? Because I am drama-driven, therefore only a hospital can fill the bill, comes the reply.

Joyous hours, these are. But wait, the fun is only beginning. I am now the father of children by three different mothers: clearly, I am the father of chaos, and am financially irresponsible. I am an animal. I mean, my parents are aging rapidly, and here in this time of their greatest need, what have I been up to?

"Now why don't you tell our studio audience about your financial concerns?" Oh my arrogance, what a hole I've dug, cancelling out my health insurance because my mind told me that we were beyond the need for modern medicine, and I had wanted to believe it.

"But dig deep, sucker and tell us the whole story." All right, if you'll just loosen my collar for a sec, I'll come clean. Yeah, I wanted a baby girl, not because I don't have any, but because I didn't want to face the circumcision issue, because I didn't want to have to speak my truth. I knew that I couldn't subject my son to a circumcision, a newborn male's initiation into the order of sacrifice and separation, as I had done with the other boys.

The voices continue, ad nauseam. But I am present enough to not push the chorus away to fester somewhere in my body. I realize that it must run its course, and my intent is to release it, not to bury or buy it. So, I respond by going home for a while and getting what I need in the form of support from family and friends, sleep, and Tai Chi.

The voices of self-hate do eventually run their course, and a deep happiness slowly emerges, one that feels filled with the promise of a life beyond the guilt-driven existence I have followed until so recently. I return to the hospital renewed and ready to bring my loved ones home.

From the instant that we are in the house and I am holding my child, I feel me as I have never felt myself. I discover my pure state when I fall asleep with him lying on my chest, and I sink into a deep place that simply is, free of any agenda, including dreams. I experience this even while watching a televised basketball game, cradling him in my arms. I can be fully immersed in material reality, and simultaneously be aware of the essence of my life will, so clear to me now from our connection.

These first days of his life are, for me, not about adjusting to a new person, but about feeling more complete, more fully me than I have ever felt. I recognize him, I recognize his energy, not as from a previous lifetime, but rather as in an energy sphere I have known all my life and that has just taken a leap by claiming fragments of itself, a manifestation of my desire to be free. He is our gift, acknowledgement that we are more here and now each day. He sees Mary and me at our cores, just as I do with others in my work, and he holds that space for us, wholeheartedly. When I am with him I cannot help but return to myself.

When the other boys were newborn, although I did not say so, I always felt somewhat uncomfortable and out of touch, as I was still deep in a world of separation, and so I looked forward to their more rational days, when they would join me in that domain.

Now, I could not ask for tomorrow. Gone is the frustration, the karma of days past. I am increasingly magnetized by the now. I follow my heart homeward. My family is alive, and yet I want more: I pictured all of my children gathered around for his arrival, and the truth is that it was not time for this alignment to occur. They are strong reflections of the dispersion, born into the momentum of the sacrificial way, yet all capable of healing the inner split. I am not all the way home yet, although I have caught sight of it, and I dedicate myself to this end, and of course to handing this gift to my boys.

And so appears this beautiful child, whose name is Kahlieh (pronounced Kah-lee-eh), a reflection of my self-love, of my connection to the divine, and with his manifestation arises my desire to heal all of my fragments, to prioritize and to act upon this desire, in this lifetime, at this juncture. All else will follow. No longer do I choose to exist within the sacrificial paradigm. My spirit is alive, regardless of the demons.

In the Jaws of Kanagi*

In the days and weeks following Kahlieh's birth, we savor our newborn, putting my practice closure and our move to the mountains on the back burner. He appears bright and healthy. Already, I carry him in the sling for walks on the trails; here and on Mary's breast are where he is happiest. Slowly, we address the endings before us.

Meanwhile, Aaron and Dylan temporarily move back in and use our home as a base for their transition into summer doings. The place begins to feel unsettled. On June 5, Kahlieh turns ill. A darkness, almost palpable, descends into the house.

---

* "Kanagi" is a symbolic name for the material-scientific civilization we are now in.

June 7. 3 A.M. Kahlieh is still sick. It began two nights ago with vomiting, followed by a fever. Tonight, the fever has broken, but he cannot sleep, and he is hurting.

These nights are a throwback to twelve years ago with my premature newborn Mikael, when night after night for two years, I would bring him to his mother for feeding several times each night. During the day, I worked myself mercilessly into the ground. I turned into a walking zombie back then.

My greatest fear with our new baby has been of sleepless nights while I am still treating. Hours from now I will begin my final work week here. This was supposed to have been my last day, before tomorrow's new moon, but I succumbed to money fears and so am stretching it out for a couple more days.

I'm aware of something increasingly ominous in the house. So much activity, so much doing, by Aaron, Dylan, and us, in preparing for our changes. I also believe that my leaving this town is creating some anxiety for these two, since I have anchored us here for five years.

I have chosen to not treat Kahlieh because I believe that in times past I doctored my children at the expense of parenting them. But yesterday, I discovered a small black-and-blue mark at one of the most important acupuncture points on his body. It is a point I frequently use in treating chronic, acute conditions; it relates to blood circulation and production and to the healing capacity for the entire body. Translated from the Japanese, the name of the point has a number of interpretations, including "stuck inside," "deep hidden place," and "incurable problems." Since I saw the mark, which is coming from the inside out, I have grown increasingly troubled.

June 7. 4 A.M. I awaken again to Kahlieh's crying. I instinctively take him to my chest and will hold him here until morning. Then, something extraordinary occurs: I have the clear sense of a divine presence having entered my hands. I have never felt this. I do nothing but continue to hold him, while this energy is at work. Over the last three years I have worked exclusively with my hands when treating my patients, so I have had plenty of opportunity to observe what hands-on healing feels like. But what I am witnessing here is beyond my grasp. I remain aware of the energy transmission as I drift into sleep. A unique calm flows into me, and my concerns about Kahlieh soon evaporate.

June 7. 7 A.M. I awaken feeling rested, thinking that surely he will get well this day. Mary has been feeling on edge through his illness, but this morning, she is looking calmer. I leave for work, concerned that endings there today will demand my attention.

June 7. 8:20 A.M. I arrive at my wonderful treatment room, a cozy space that looks out at the mountains. The office is graced by cards and potted plants, reflections of my patients' gratitude.

I reflect on how free from guilt I am in ending my practice. The closures are approaching my ideal, in that they are devoid of hidden strings and done in respect to the people I have treated. I believe in my patients' individual capacities to bring the healing to fruition, and even if symptoms still remain, they now have the tools for the rest of the journey. For myself, increasingly I no longer need any of them to validate me, and I see how this makes me free to act on behalf of the truth.

The morning calls in people at various stages of healing, including one who may not live much longer. My sentiment resides in a more sober place than in years past, when I would have tried to do more for people who kept getting sicker. In fact, there was a time when my greed to heal was such that I would have put off closing my practice until I had "fixed" a deeply ill patient's symptoms or until the person died. Today, I happily stand nearer to the appropriateness of what is mine to give. I have done my part for the woman who may die, and now as I close with her I accept whatever her life will may choose.

At morning's end, I see a patient who exhibits a rare desire to go all the way for her healing, and I get the feeling that our paths will cross again.

I sense that my work is about to metamorphose and likely will change form. The funny part of this practice, call it acupuncture, is that the principle it is based on was never intended to be limited to this field: my teacher created this form of acupuncture so that his students could make a living while studying the underlying Life Principle. The treatment room has been a great place to practice--it gives a form to the pursuit of our personal realization, via the one-to-one life mirror, in a laboratory setting. It was true for me.

Today, fifteen years down this road, I believe there are more efficient, joyous, and expansive ways to transmit and to pursue our full healing than in this context. Too much work, lacking in dignity, and ultimately stifling. Perhaps, in the space that is being created by ending this practice, I will discover these.

On that note, I'll make a quick jaunt home to check on my loved ones.

June 7. 2 P.M. Kahlieh was sleeping when I arrived home, and Mary's gaunt face reflected her lack of sleep.

Several days ago, when he got sick, I went on a run and asked myself what the reflection of his illness was for me. The answer I received was that I was carrying home sickness from the office: "Ja Ki," Japanese for bad energy, is one of the greatest hazards of my occupation. We all carry it, and it is released in great quantities during a treatment. Over the years, I have brought home every condition imaginable, on one occasion or another. Ja Ki comes directly to the practitioner in big helpings when he/she believes that he/she is the one doing the healing. What came clear to me on the run is that I had spent too many years working with the stuff. As a result, I had become more vulnerable, and now the poison is leaking into my home. Funny, for many years I couldn't understand why more people didn't want to do this work.

Recent insights such as this have supported me in feeling free to move on. Doubtless, it is the right time.

Not everyone thinks so. My next patient would like me to treat her till the end of days. I sense how she wants our goodbye to be more gooey, so that she might call me back in to treat her after her next undoing. I like feeling the severity of my observation: it's a window on impeccability and ultimately my freedom.

Gratefully, I see this treatment day come to a close.

June 7. 6 P.M. I am not one to be easily surprised--
I was born on the full moon in Pisces. I can hear what
others are *considering* thinking. But I am surprised, no
shocked to the point of denial, at what awaits me: Mary
is holding Kahlieh, who lies in a state of trance. Dylan
is standing beside her. They appear mystified by
Kahlieh's behavior and emit a strange, giddy edge that
hinges on humorous.

I go to the bathroom. When I return, his left side is
moving in slow-motion convulsions. I work on
Kahlieh, and the convulsions stop, but he does not come
all the way back. He is still off somewhere.

We have to do something, so we agree to go to the
well--to take him for a walk on a trail, since he always
relaxes there. Underlying our decision, I am faced with
an unfamiliar feeling. I have worked on a loved one
who had fallen on a supermarket floor with a heart at-
tack, on a child of mine at the extreme edge of asthmatic
breathing, on my premature newborn, on anaphylactic
shock in one of my children, on appendicitis in another,
and on tumors and cancers in my relatives. I worked on
them unhesitatingly from a place of deep confidence.
Nowadays, it usually takes me little time to diagnose a
condition and to decide on a treatment strategy. But
from the instant I make contact with him, I feel certain
that help for Kahlieh's current condition lies outside of
my abilities.

As it turns out, the walk is for Mary and me to see reality. Even on the trail, the darkness we were feeling in the house surrounds us. We agree that we need to act quickly.

8 P.M. I call an M.D. acquaintance whose judgment I respect. He gently but firmly confirms that it's time for modern medicine and that we should get to a hospital. Mary simultaneously calls one of the midwives who stood by us at Kahlieh's birth. She recommends the same action and offers to join us immediately.

Driving to the local hospital, I have no business being behind the wheel, as my weeping turns into a wail. Mary holds him for all she is worth, and pleads with him to come back. We are journeying deeper into the darkness.

Once Kahlieh is inside the emergency room, the cutting, puncturing, taking of blood, X-rays, and injections begin. The on-call doctor feels uncomfortable having us in the room, since we are paying close attention to his every action.

From the start, we are clear that we have come as Kahlieh's advocates. Having assumed this responsibility, we will be forced to become increasingly empty, in order to hear what Kahlieh wants, as opposed to any ideas that we may have. It will ultimately mean letting go of any agendas and suspending all judgment that we carry from outside the present moment. Simple: at this, the most stressful time of our lives, we call upon ourselves to stand in naka-ima, the here and now, like we never have. This does not mean stiff upper lip and stick our feelings in our gut. To the contrary, it means being fully awake and alive, in touch with all feelings. Naka-ima is the place where our apriori essence, which exists in the creative void of no-form, and our phenomenal aposteriori self, which exists in material reality, merge into one simultaneous expression; this place of synchronicity is the Garden of Eden in all of us, as opposed to the paradigm of separation, the constant mode of reaction from which we have created the material-scientific civilization. It certainly does not happen in an instant, but the greatest transformation of my life begins to occur in this starlight world.

Meanwhile, back in the emergency room, I question the doctor's intended procedure, and he immediately turns big with me. I just as quickly call him on his attitude, telling him that it feels like a steamroller. He backs down, but this is only the beginning.

Having served as an emergency medical technician, I can't believe my eyes with the incompetence in this room. There are no successful first attempts at getting I.V.'s hooked up, at drawing blood, or at getting breathing support going. And they do not even act to keep my baby warm. Kahlieh's blood flows freely with each procedure. We are informed that he has suffered a cerebral hemorrhage. All that the doctor keeps offering is, "You have a very sick baby."

He blames the illness on the fact that I rejected a Vitamin K shot for Kahlieh at birth (later proven to be a premature and false diagnosis). At this and at their incompetence, I get angry, turn frustrated, feel shamed. Immediately, I witness my power drain, and I assume the familiar role of victim.

I head for the waiting room, where my mind immediately goes into self-survival mode. I feel Kahlieh dying. Here in this chamber of terror, my mind tracks my life with Mary. From the start, it reasons, she and I were set up in a cosmic power play. We got together from our greater alignment, rather than from true romance. Then, quickly and contrary to all precaution, she was pregnant. Little matter at this moment that our pregnancy and his birth had already been my redemption. I am feeling the depth of his condition, and I hate that I can't fix it, that it's beyond my control. All I can do is scream, "What the fuck, God?"

But the rage grows, because for me, the emergency room is the last straw. After all, I practice Life Medicine, which is dedicated to returning the balance to our way with life on this planet. "What the fuck, then, am *I* doing in an emergency room?"

All I know is that it sucks, that it is humiliating. We do not have insurance, because I wanted to believe that we did not need it. All that I can see is the existence I created spiraling down the tubes.

Abandoned by God, perhaps, but not not by my mind--it is fighting like never before, promising to soothe my predicament, to fix my suffering. I am reminded that there is a woman out there, waiting for me. Although I've never met her, I somehow know her, even fell in love with her a few months ago. God, it was intoxicating. I strongly sense her again now and feel certain that she will take my pain away, that she will welcome me back home.

And then I will have to pay.

When I am on the edge, I run for a woman. When am I on the edge? When I go into my head, turning over-rational, over-yang. I then separate from my yin-- my feminine, feeling body. When I live in my head I become out of touch, and am therefore in danger. To survive at this juncture, I look outwards for what I've abandoned inside of me. I try to fix what I have overriden. But on such a course, I remain in separation from my full being. Hence, the suffering.

Even here, in this waiting room of the hell world, my feelings from beyond separation show up to break the spell. My truth is that this time I will not buy a ticket back, no matter what I am faced with. At once I am

ashamed and intrigued by my mind's course. I am glad
that I did not censor it.

A key to not walking my mind's way, I discover, is
to not indulge in feeling sorry for myself, because as
soon as I do, I vacate, leave the space, and sure enough
someone will step in to make the decisions. Besides, I
spent much of my life feeling angry and powerless--no,
wait--the truth is, I actually felt almost nothing. I begin
to breathe again, and soon enough my intention to stay in
the now and not abandon myself is secure.

When I return to the emergency room, I learn that the
decision has been made to transfer Kahlieh to the best
hospital in the area for his condition. Thank goodness!

June 8. The ambulance transports us in the wee
hours of the morning, with Kahlieh encased in a support
system, while we observe him going still further away.
When we arrive at the hospital, the attendants ask us to
wait outside the infant intensive care unit while they get
him settled. Mary and I find a vacant lounge with a pull-
out sleeper. Then, with the midwives, Aaron, and Dylan
standing guard in the waiting room, we go crashing into
sleep.

I hear a voice coming from somewhere in the
darkness and I struggle to connect with it. It is talking to
us, but I do not recognize it and I do not know where we
are. I feel my body shaking from head to toe, uncon-

trollably, as if freezing, but I'm not. The gentle but persistent voice is making a monumental request: it tells us that Kahlieh needs a blood transfusion. I am a Doctor of Life Medicine. I strive to practice non-violence, to honor the essence of all living things. To that end, I even stopped using needles, since they are a form of surgery. I have practiced the belief that destroying any form of natural life is tantamount to destroying the truth. I believe that when modern medicine shocks the body, the body is cellularly altered. We pay the price for any invasive procedure, of this I have no doubt. But what I believe does not make her request go away.

Right off the bat, we stand face to face with the possibility of polluted blood being passed into our child, let alone the energetic consequences of *someone else's blood coming into his body*. The gentle voice belongs to a doctor who tells us that time is of the essence; Kahlieh needs the blood now. When her voice fades, I fight off the desire to go back to sleep. I check in, searching how I feel beyond the shock and the exhaustion. I do not fear his dying. Good, my motive will not come from there. The message I receive is that Kahlieh needs blood. Mary gets the same message. Just as we get it, the doctor returns, and Mary and I sign the release form.

Soon, we are allowed to see Kahlieh. There is our not-even-ten-pound baby lying in a cart. He does not look real. Breathing support is crammed down his throat, I.V.s for food and for arresting convulsions are attached to his arm and to his head, and there is a catheter jammed up his penis, so he gives the appearance of having a constant erection. His dull facial sheen tells the story.

Not the whole story, since at this point we believe that he has separated from his body and is looking things over from a place apart. Of this, Mary and I feel certain: his life will has detached while he decides whether to stay or to go. Mary and I continue to transmit our care but we are primarily committed at this juncture to honoring his life will. To this end, we are careful not to tug on him and plead with him to stay. I am astonished at my detachment. At times I judge myself on this for being callous: I must be numb. But my truth is that in my past, fear, sadness, and hidden rage are all that ever propelled me. As I stand beside my child, I am more free, ever-closer to the source. Now, the earth is beginning to feel round. Over the next 24 hours, Kahlieh slowly but surely returns to his body.

In the moment-to-moment of this time, ideas and beliefs I held reveal themselves as stick figures-- inanimate--each and every one a false idol. In turn, I begin to release them, one by one. I will cling to some longer than others, but my devotion to the here and now sooner or later renders them dead. After a while, I can almost see them, as some ancient mummified fetishes, that have just been exposed to sunlight: they begin to disintegrate into dust.

The environment and the situation become our mentors. Just outside the automated swinging doors of the I.C.U., I discover other fathers in the parents' lounge. They spend their time eating junk food, drinking coffee, reading newspapers, or channel surfing the T.V. Most of them will stay for no more than a day or two, while some never show up. I am not tempted to join them, since twelve years ago, I chose that road.

This time, I am walking through it alive. I have no place to go and, suddenly, nothing to do, outside of being with Kahlieh and Mary. It is a major accomplishment to eat good food each day, to shower, and to do the laundry. I find myself busy addressing the rage, the grief, the fear, the anxiety, the joy, and ultimately, the emptiness, as they arise. I am careful to not indulge the feelings. And as if this were not enough, around every corner lie one or more of the intensive care team, wanting to do this or that. Their call is usually for more procedures, which translates into more invasion.

Then, in this most extreme sanctum of the material-scientific civilization, something remarkable begins to happen. The M.D.s soon see that they cannot dictate every decision to us and that fear is not Mary's and my motive vibration. And strange as we may act, they respect us. So together, we all slowly join in a voyage through a suspended moment, to a place where our disparate paradigms struggle to meet and to find a common language. After all, it's about Kahlieh.

Only two days later, thanks to artificial breathing support that has hyperventilated him, the circumference of Kahlieh's head continues to decrease, a sign that he is normalizing. Mary starts nursing him again, and he is quickly moving off all support systems. The doctors tell us that he can be released in two days--all that they will need is a series of X-rays from head to toe, to verify that he was not beaten. Standard operating procedure, state requirement. Crap! Fill this child with radiation to prove our innocence. I go outside to release my rage at the world that we have created. Meanwhile, Mary, anchored by my friend and colleague Paul, stays with Kahlieh, allowing me this freedom to separate from the scene. Only when I have released my anger can I begin to address the M.D.s' request. Mary and I agree to seek out an advocate to see if we can avoid the X-rays. Strange new partners (us) these doctors have called in: our attitude clearly is not in the name of convenience. So most likely, Kahlieh will not be released in two days, since our research will take time, and tomorrow is the weekend.

Although Mary is feeling great excitement at his resurgence, deep down I am in touch with a truth-- Kahlieh's disposition to the illness has not been healed.

His improvement is due to a temporary fix. In this
moment, I hate my seeing.

Tonight, I consult an oracle, something I rarely do
these days, to ask about Kahlieh's illness. I throw the I
Ching, or "The Book of Changes." In a nutshell, the
message is that although in this hexagram heaven is
above earth and they appear to be in their proper order,
they are going in opposite directions, as expressions of
their natural energies: yang is going up, while yin is
going down. Therefore, there is no intercourse between
the two primary energies of life. The result is
"Misfortune," since a blockage is created and energy is
therefore stagnating. The lines of the hexagram then
change into "Retreat," a scenario where the positive
energy is retreating while the negative energy is
advancing--our possible future. As I hold Kahlieh and
feel his next wave of illness coming, I ponder what the
reflection of the "I Ching" throw is for me. Is the
swelling in his head a karmic reflection of my arrogance,
of my cleverness, of my living in my head, separated
from my body and my feelings? Is he reflecting the
separation of male and female, of heaven and earth, of
light and shadow, being manifested across the board on
this planet? I grow tired with the thoughts.

The next day, his head circumference again begins to
increase. His imbalance is now attributed to
hydrocephalus, the inability to properly drain cere-

brospinal fluid. It is explained that we each create three times more fluid than we need every day, and that the excess is normally absorbed by villi in our heads. We are told that his hemorrhage was an intraventricular bleed, which damaged the villi and put them out of proper working order, at least for the time being. With nowhere to go, the cerebrospinal fluid stays in the head and puts increasing pressure on the brain. For a time, we are told, the swelling can occur without causing permanent damage.

A nurse, seeing that Mary intends to stay with Kahlieh around the clock, finds us a small room inside the I.C.U. We gladly accept it. I feel certain that time is of the essence if we are to turn the tide without further intervention. I see this room as a window of opportunity: I can work on him safely in here. The doctors want to do a comparison CT Scan, taking one picture, then injecting fluid into his head for the second one. I tell them I need time to see if my work can do it, that we do not want to subject him to further invasion if at all possible. They go off to huddle and soon return telling us that they will not interfere and will support us however they can. Then, we all agree to a time frame. After they leave, Mary and I look at each other in wonder at what has just happened.

Over the next ten days, we will rarely leave this room. Kahlieh cries full force much of the time. The three of us sleep in a slightly oversized single bed to the backdrop of frequent emergency alarms notifying nurses of the status of twenty other newborns outside our door. There are AIDS-infected babies, babies with heart diseases, and heroine-addicted babies. Some are getting the only love and attention they will ever experience-- from dedicated nurses.

We are living in an emergency room in the decaying heart of this city, bordering epidemic homelessness and extreme violence. None of this affects our actions. And even though I am treating him, we are not trying to prove something. We keep our eyes on a ball called reality.

Meanwhile, our life here gets transmitted to the outside world via a calling tree established for nightly updates. Support pours in from a group of people aligned by the irresistible being of a six-week-old child who speaks from the heart and who I begin to suspect is mirroring the condition of our world at a critical turning point. The attention grows exponentially, from people who have never met him: an entire little league team runs up to a mother after each practice to find out how "the baby" is; before going off to play, a group of little girls first asks the same question of a mother in-the-know.

Generosity pours in. Wonderful, deeply nourishing meals are prepared and delivered, at times complete with china and tablecloth. A former patient declares that she is taking over our house packing, as well as delegating people to support us at the hospital. They appear whenever we begin to falter, and support us appropriately. When my efforts with Kahlieh begin to stall out, practitioners from other disciplines volunteer to come in and work on him.

Inside the unit, we talk with the staff about my work and about our cosmology. One late night, I sit in the conference room with a baffled doctor, who is still without understanding of what caused the hemorrhage and wants to know how I see it.

On a rainy Saturday afternoon in the thick of our struggle to bring him through, Mary and I are once more informed of how many people are praying for Kahlieh. Suddenly, I realize that these prayers are working against him, in that Mary and I have been feeling something else flooding into the room: in reality, these people, however well-wishing they may be, have also been transmitting their pain to him. We immediately send out a request that everyone concerned claim whatever feelings that may be arising from his illness as their own. We ask them to employ these feelings, to search them out for their personal healing. We see how Kahlieh's pain can evoke the victim in all of us, and we have no desire to perpetuate that. Soon after we make our request, things begin to feel cleaner.

Later that day, I stand in the hospital laundry room folding our clothes with Kahlieh's godmother, Katy, who is also a Life Medicine doctor, when we look up at one another at the same instant with a recognition: "This is what we've worked for, the time that we've been waiting for," I declare.

"Yes," she grins broadly, "we are beginning to come alive, and right here of all places."

We've been awaiting our acceptance of an unknown, a frontier that lies inside each of us. It cannot be made manifest, be seen phenomenally, until we make contact and reawaken from our sleep.

The catch is that there are no promises of what we will find there, no guarantees. Only our hunger and courage to find out can carry us through the fears. To become like a salmon and swim against the current for the journey home. A primal, ancient promise that we made to ourselves.

As we approach our agreed-to deadline for Kahlieh's improvement, the depth of his illness is revealed. Each day his head circumference remains the same or slowly expands, and I start to contract. One night, my patience collapses when a doctor brings in some interns and declares that we need to act soon, since we are approaching the danger zone. I feel angry because she is pushing us and has violated the sanctity of the agreement that they would support us. Now, she is bringing the language of "what if" into the room, the language of fear. She knows that we are still within safe bounds and that we have not for a moment compromised Kahlieh's well-being. I am also angry because I know what procedure lies ahead, even though they have been dancing around it--the implantation of a V-P shunt. And I have not yet come to terms with it. After making a quick trip to the bathroom to yell and scream in private, I return and immediately insist that the doctor and her cronies leave the room.

As my fuse shortens, Mary's light shines more brightly, thereby giving me space to pace and to fret, to rage, to think, and to draw diagrams attempting to solve Kahlieh's illness. Friends and acquaintances are taken with her being. I see her best when she is breastfeeding Kahlieh: each moment she remains clear of her path, which is simply her dedication to return to the one source. Standing in this clarity, she does not commit sacrifice, even to her child.

The next morning, while taking a rare break from our room, we are informed that we will need to vacate the room. They offer a much smaller room, where there is no space for me. We are told that our belongings are being removed as we speak. I break into uncontrollable laughter, for I had devised a method to not leave the room, even to go to the bathroom, during these increasingly difficult nights. To that end, I peed in a jar, which I had not yet emptied this morning. I suddenly saw it as my contribution to the dissolution of the uneasy partnership we had formed with the hospital staff.

Coincident with vacating our room, I realize that my treatments are not going to do it now for Kahlieh. On this day, we give the M.D.s permission to try to drain some fluid by tapping into his head, through his brain to the swelled ventricle below. They think that perhaps this procedure will do it, but inside I know that a shunt is called for.

A shunt is a valve and flexible tube combination that is surgically placed in the head ventricles, then pushed under the skin down to the peritoneal cavity, where it drains in with similar substances in the stomach.

As the inevitability of the procedure approaches, I imagine my Life Medicine teacher laughing at the notion and exclaiming that in a human being, cerebrospinal fluid does not drain into the peritoneal cavity. While his teachings have touched me deeply, this ultimately strikes me as one more idea to release, albeit the most formidable I have faced.

Because what I have really been *listening to* is Kahlieh's desire, the final decision is easy. In the days that I treated him, I ultimately saw, beyond the shadow of a doubt, that his energetic tendency to the imbalance is so great that we will need support to buy time for the greater healing, and that he will, at this juncture, die without the shunt. I feel certain that he wants to be here. The shunt, then, will serve as our bridge.

The M.D.s call it permanent, since they've never seen one removed in a condition like his. I see it as temporary, a device to relieve the pressure and to help him recover and get strong, while we heal the energetic that created the disease.

So now, we ready ourselves for the surgery, scheduled for tomorrow night.

At dinner time, while friends hold Kahlieh, Mary and I retreat to a courtyard surrounded by beautiful flowers. But we do not retreat from our reality. As we eat, we once again search the cause of his condition. We have already tracked it back to conception and before. We worked hard to make the pregnancy as healthy as it could be. We did not do it perfectly. Kahlieh has his agenda, too. We track it all once again. Before he got really sick, Mary and I had already begun to grasp what a mirror Kahlieh holds for us. Tonight, what surfaces above all else is that the time has come for our own healing.

"I accept responsibility for whatever I may have done," Mary says, "but right now this does not matter. What matters to me is that the time has come to pull out the stops, to dedicate ourselves to our full emergence, from this moment on, no compromise."

In response, I confess something that I have been slow to claim: "I see that our not having health insurance was an act of delusion."

This spoken, I join her in this dedication.

June 20. 6:30 P.M. Summer solstice--the day of greatest sun--arrives tomorrow morning. A soft rain has begun to fall. I have gone through this day knowing that the surgery is going to go well. Family and friends have been with us all day. Moreover, there has been a steadily increasing inpouring of support from those who are not here. Now, the walls of Kahlieh's room feel like they are pulsing with the attention. It has felt good, all day.

I am alone now with Kahlieh. Soon, they will take him. His effect on me has been unprecedented and unpredictable. His pain has shattered all remnants of my life-as-Day-Timer existence. I move more free from agenda each moment. Even now, I glimpse a being beyond bounds, steeped in a knowing that for me is but a glimmer. He offers new possibilities to everyone. He is a lot to be contained in human form; perhaps his illness reflects some of this. I cannot say if he is more exceptional than any other child; I can only say that I have been receptive.

Too soon, the staff wheels him toward surgery. Mary and I walk as far as they will allow us to accompany him. As we part, he looks at us with terror in his eyes, later noted in his chart as "extreme anxiety."

Mary and I join Katy, Paul, and another friend, who brings us dinner. Per our request, she brought tuna, and I can see her puzzlement about the non-vegetarian selection. I explain that we need some density tonight in order to harmonize with our environment. We are prepared for a two-hour surgery.

Mary, finally free to collapse, reveals, "I could not have gone on for another minute."

I observe that her timing is impeccable.

Our talk is sober. Forty minutes later, we are told that surgery went well and that we are free to see our baby.

Kahlieh has chosen to live. I am being sprung from the logistical web of survival that I created out of my fear-based existence. My one anchor is that I feel compelled to tell the story. I no longer recognize myself, an at once alarming and deeply intriguing reality.

Tonight, Mary and I are going home, to sleep in our bed, while Katy stays beside Kahlieh, who is not allowed to nurse until morning. We walk arm-in-arm into the rain-blessed evening air, when I am suddenly transported back to my earliest childhood memory:

I am six weeks old, just like Kahlieh, and I
am being transported in an ambulance to this
hospital. I have the croup. I cannot breathe.

I am captivated by the lights of a carnival,
close to the hospital entrance.

On that night, I was reflecting something severely out of balance in our family's relation to one another, as well as in my relation to life on this planet. My parents reacted that night by pushing harder in the same direction, and my life only turned tighter.

This time around, when we arrived here in the ambulance with Kahlieh, we could not see where our lives or that of our newborn child were going, but we committed to stay in the moment as fully as we were able, to empty out, and to embrace our multi-dimensional being. We committed to standing in naka-ima, the time and place of the existence of truth.

Tonight, on the threshold of our healing, everything is different. We are walking into a new life.

Afterword

Last week, while I was deeply engaged in the writing of my last story, I received a call from my former wife, telling me that my Life Principle teacher, O Sensei M.M. Nakazono, had died. Deep down, I already knew this, so what I experienced more than grief was a vast emptiness, a space waiting to be filled. The torch had been passed. There was no more "they" either to push up against or to hold onto. In an instant, my time had arrived.

I immediately got sick. For days, I lay in bed devoid of energy, feeling toxins moving slowly down from head to toes. It so happens that my intention for the new moon only three days before he died had been to claim who I am, fully. What I observed in bed was my self-hate. Opposition, fragmentation, all creating energy drain, all manifesting as poison.

The border guards had pulled me aside and were interrogating me: Was this book the product of a dangerously devious and demented mind? A paranoic fantasy? I struggled to breathe, to remain centered, as their vicious dogs prepared to make me their lunch.

Birthing this book into the world called in doubts from the far reaches of my soul; at the core lay my fear of being perceived as arrogant, as well as questioning my soul's purpose. Never would I have guessed that it would be so demanding to let go. What a gift to do so.

In closing, I would like to relate a custom from my Life Medicine school: Each evening, to signify that class had come to an end, Sensei Nakazono would, in his beautifully inflected Japanese accent, say, "So, we stop here for now." Then, he would bow to us and say, "Thank You."

In turn, the class would bow to him and reply, "Thank you, Sensei."

Now, my time has come to acknowledge this remarkable soul. Sensei, you were a man before your time, walking a lonely and difficult path. I treasure your transmission. Thank you, Sensei. I dedicate this book to your living spirit.

Appendix:
Introduction to Kototama Life Medicine and the Life Principle

I was first introduced to Kototama Life Medicine during the summer of 1977, while attending an intensive with its founder, Masahilo M. Nakazono. In 1978, Sensei Nakazono opened the Kototama Institute's School of Kototama Life Medicine, where I enrolled a year later.

Life Medicine is an extraordinary system of healing. And yet, the medicine is but one application of the underlying Life Principle. The truest and deepest healing occurs when one begins to apply the Life Principle in daily life.

The Life Principle
The Life Principle is, in a sentence, an understanding that human life is created, maintained, and destroyed based

upon a specific order of fifty sound vibrations emanating from the void. Call it the newest of the "New Physics," but it is actually an ancient way that we are only beginning to grasp. As our understanding of the principle grows, we will see how we do indeed create our world through our words, thoughts, emotions, and actions, all of which are simply energetic manifestations of the fifty sounds.

Within each of us, the fifty sound vibrations divide into five currents of energy, or meridians (one more than modern physics' four-dimensional reality). These five dimensions are what make us human. It is only when we are properly engaging each of these capacities that we can say we are being fully human:

1) Spiritual, the A (as in "ah") -Wa dimension, which separates into the following levels of activity: emotion, imagination, intuition, universal spirit, and inspiration, in that order.

2) Life will, the I (as in "ee") -Wi dimension.

3) Judgment, the E (as in "eh") -We dimension.

4) Memory and knowledge, including karma, the O (as in "oh") -Wo dimension.

5) The five physical senses, the U (as in "ooh") -Wu dimension, which separate into seeing, hearing, smelling, tasting, and touching.

The fifty sounds also create all word forms. When we speak, we are "practicing" the sounds, however unconsciously. The sounds can be intentionally practiced in their pure form by saying each sound separately. Sounding them as mantras does not work. By practicing the sounds in a particular order, by listening to our voices as we do, and by feeling the sounds arise from the tanden, or creative void center of the body (located about an inch below the navel), we can experience the nature of each sound and its creative force.

Life Medicine

Life Medicine was founded as a way to bring the Life Principle into action for the benefit of health practitioner and patient. It encompasses sound exercises and physical handwork, diet treatment, exercise treatment, lifestyle treatment, and acupuncture treatment.

Life Medicine differs from the standard five-element theory of acupuncture in a most fundamental way. Traditional acupuncture is based upon the principle of Amatu Kanagi, the way of the material-scientific civilization. At the center of this paradigm lies the dimension of our five physical senses, the U-Wu dimension, which has guided our search to perfect materiality. Life Medicine, on the other hand, is based upon the order of Amatu Futonolito, which goes beyond the scientific-material civilization to a more complete expression of human life. At the heart of this search lies the dimension of our judgment from a space of non-attachment, the E-We dimension. In the realm of Kototama Life Medicine, the five dimensions are not perceived as they are in Traditional Oriental Medicine: the five elements of wood, fire, earth, metal, and water. Instead, they represent the above-stated dimensions of human life, which flow through the body as currents of energy.

Life Medicine diagnosis and treatment identifies which current has lost synchronization or balance with the others, or which parts of the body are out of harmony with the rest. The medicine works to maintain the highest possible condition of circulation of the five apriori dimensions' energy within the space of the human body. It addresses life at the level of no-form, the realm of apriori, seeking to balance the disposition at its creative source. From here, the healing moves out to the rest of the body and into form, or aposteriori.

The Healing Process

We can apply Life Medicine and the Life Principle to achieve the degree of healing we desire. On the most basic level, we can rely on Life Medicine treatments to relieve our symptoms. Or, we can take more responsibility for our well-being and place treatments in their truest role: as support while we make the lifestyle changes necessary for ongoing good health. To heal at the deepest level, we can search for the root causes of an illness, by looking at the five-fold components of the condition, and begin applying the Life Principle to all aspects of our life. The ultimate goal in such an effort is to bring all aposteriori phenomenon into alignment with our apriori intentions. In other words, our inner and outer worlds become a unified whole.

Once we apply the Life Principle wholeheartedly, the flow of our life energy moves to the beat of an entirely different drummer. In this new energy configuration, the center of our universe actually becomes redefined. Instead of seeking experiences and then reacting to them, as in U-Wu, we act from the void center, and everything else in our life follows.

This shift in our foundation from U-Wu to E-We changes our relationship to the universe. From the viewpoint of U-Wu, we are the object of outside forces acting upon us. When we shift to the viewpoint of E-We, we become the subject, creating our life from pure intention. Gone is the powerless victim as we begin to merge into a world at once alive and for which we are clearly responsible. Herein lies the seed of a new civilization.

Bibliography

Dawson, Louis W. II. *Colorado 10th Mountain Trails: 10th Mountain Hut & Trail System: Official Ski Touring Guide. Aspen: WHO Press, 1989.*

Herzog, Maurice. Annapurna, First Conquest of an 8,000-Meter Peak. *New York: Dutton, 1953.*

Nakazono, Masahilo. Guide to INOCHI (Life) Medicine. *Santa Fe: Inochi Resources, 1985.*

Nakazono, Masahilo. A Guide to Natural Medicine. *Santa Fe: Kototama Institute, 1980.*

Nakazono, Masahilo. INOCHI, The Book of Life. *Santa Fe: Kototama Institute, 1979.*

Nakazono, Masahilo. Kototama Lectures. *Santa Fe: Kototama Institute, 1984.*

Nakazono, Masahilo. The Law and Therapy of Natural Life. *Santa Fe: Kototama Institute, 1980.*

Nakazono, Masahilo. My Past Way of Budo and Other Essays. *Santa Fe: Kototama Institute, 1979.*

Nakazono, Masahilo. The Real Sense of Natural Medicine. *Santa Fe: Kototama Institute, 1977.*

Nakazono, Mikoto Masahilo. The Source of the Present Civilization. *1994.*

Ogasawara, Koji. The Life Gyroscope. *Santa Fe: The Third Civilization Association, 1974.*

Ogasawara, Koji. Kototama (The Word Soul): The Principle of One Hundred Deities of the Kojiki. *Tokyo: The Third Civilization Association, 1973.*

For additional copies of *Road to Naka-Ima*,
please contact your local bookstore or order
directly from the publisher:
    Cassiquiare Press
    P.O. Box 307
    Carbondale, CO 81623

Name _______________________________________

Address ____________________________________

____

Telephone (______) ________ - ___________

For each book, include $19 plus $3 shipping
and handling; Colorado residents, add $.57
sales tax per book. Please allow 4-6 weeks
for delivery.

We welcome your comments:

____

____

____

____

____